# NORTH OF BOSTON
## *The Edge of a Warming World*

### WILLIAM SARGENT

*Cover photo by William Sargent*

# TABLE OF CONTENTS

*This book was formerly published under the title Coastal Discoveries*

# ACKNOWLEDGEMENTS

When I first started writing there were only a handful of professional photographers who specialized in natural history photography. With the advent of digital camera thousands of people can now afford to specialize in bird and animal photography.

Hundreds of them are drawn to the Plum Island Wildlife Refuge and the adjacent barrier beaches where you can witness massive migrations of birds and insects in this crucial stopover site of the East Coast flyway.

I was fortunate to be introduced to many of these photographers who have built their whole lives around being able to get out every morning before daylight, and to explore the beaches the marshes before, after, and between work at their regular jobs. It was a pleasure to get to know these dedicated and fascinating people.

I have mentioned many of them in the text. However I would like to especially thank Diane Seavey for her work on the original cover, Pete Gray for his astonishing capture of a snowy owl lunging at a Canada Goose, Steven Liffman for his photos of semi-palmated plover and Sandy Tilton for her keen eye, love of garnet sand, and sense of humor. The more pedestrian photos are all mine.

I would also like to thank Becky Coburn who has now designed covers and stewarded five of my manuscripts through the entire publication process, and my friend and inestimable editor Richard Lodge at the Newburyport Daily where many of these chapters were first published.

I would also like to thank the good people at the Quebec Labrador Foundation, The Sounds Conservancy, and the Institution for Savings, and Andy Griffith and Plum Island Outdoors for providing grants to help fund the research for this book.

And most of all I'd like to thank Kristina and Chappell for putting up with my spending long stormy nights up to my keister in cold water and long steamy days sitting on my keister typing this book in our attic, and Ben for his moral support.

# FORWARD
# Ipswich, Massachusetts
*September 2018*

*"How to get the most out of life...that is my everyday business.*
*How to extract the honey from the flower. I ramble over the*
*fields and am never so happy as when I feel myself."*
*~ Henry David Thoreau*
*1817 - 1862*

In February 2018 I finished my fourth book about Plum Island's erosion. As an environmental writer I felt I had been duty bound to discuss the effects of sea level rise on a single community. But it had been disheartening project. For every two steps forward the island made in understanding the problem scientifically, it had taken three steps backwards politically.

I needed to clear my head so I decided to embark on a series of rambles from Seabrook, New Hampshire to Gloucester, Massachusetts to investigate the natural history of this beautiful coast, and some of the people who cherish it. These then are my rambles I hope you enjoy them.

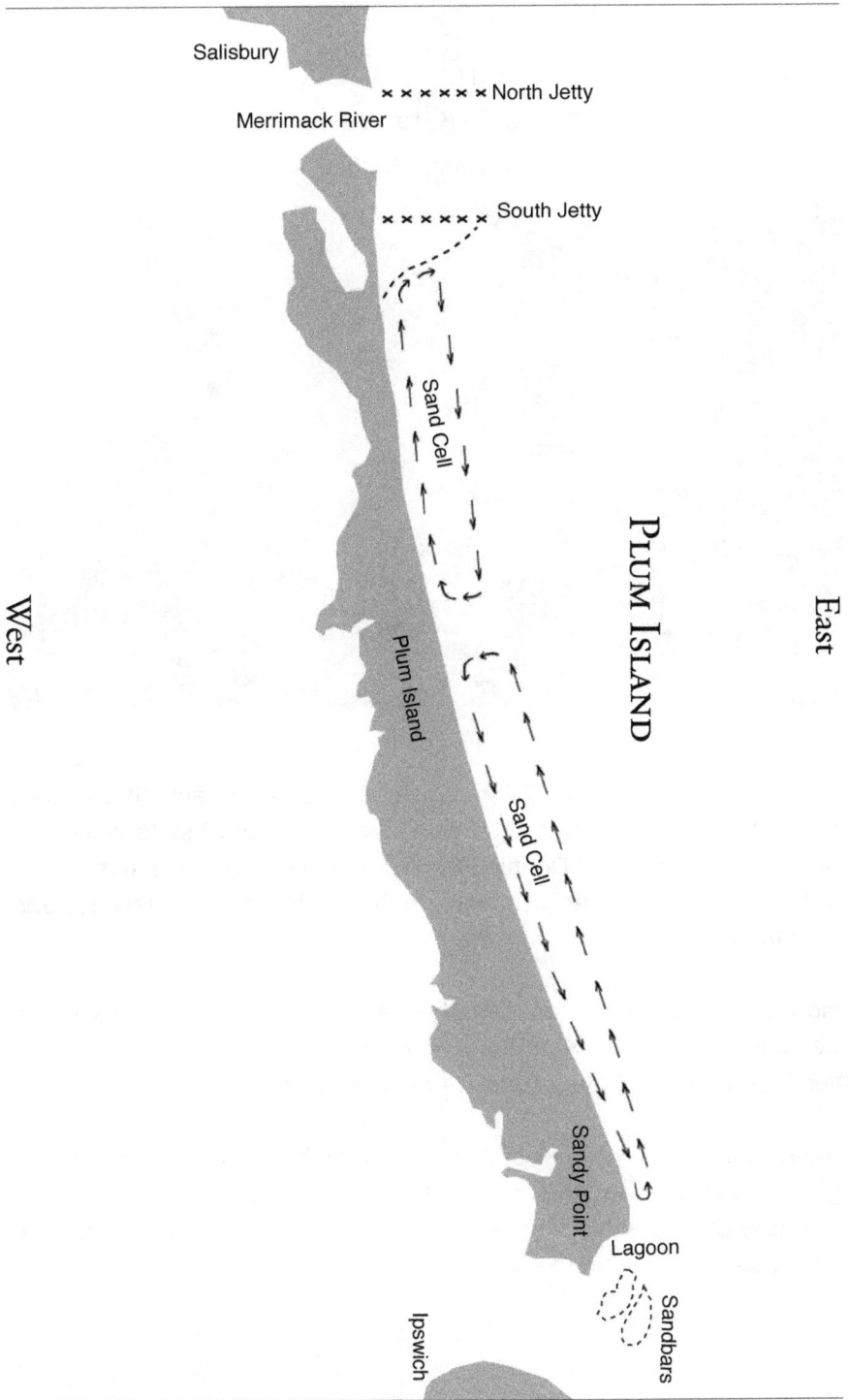

Salisbury

Merrimack River

× × × × × North Jetty

× × × × × South Jetty

Sand Cell

Plum Island

PLUM ISLAND

West

East

Sand Cell

Sandy Point

Lagoon

Sandbars

Ipswich

# CHAPTER 1
# The Seal - Crane's Beach
### *February 21, 2018*

*Seal waving.*

On February 21 Sandy Tilton drove to Crane's Beach. It was like returning home. Her father had worked at the Crane Estate when she was a girl and she and Donnie Paquin used to play on the patina green griffons that adored the lawn, explore the castle's secret passages and help themselves to food from the two large kitchens.

Now Donnie had just been loaned an office high up in the castle where he could take care of what Sandy called "her castle," "her Hog Island," "her Crane Wildlife Refuge" and "her Grande Allee."

Sandy was known for her striking photographs of patterns of erosion, garnet sand, whales, owls, shells and anything else she discovered on her daily photographic rambles. But today she wanted to just wade in the water and soak up the sun.

But soon she had dozed off and woke to a see a harbor seal sleeping beside her. As the tide came in the young seal would waddle up to be closer to her. Every time Sandy moved the seal would struggle up the beach a little further. Sandy finally decided to just stay put and the seal flopped down close enough to feel comfortable and fell asleep. They enjoyed each other's company that way for the rest of the afternoon.

When Sandy decided it was time to go home she got up and the seal dove into the water and followed her down the beach. Finally she pointed to the other side of the river and explained, "Tomorrow I'll be over there on Sandy Point. Hope to see you there!"

New England's seal population has been increasing since the early Sixties when states started to abolish their seal bounties. Seals are a necessary link in the life cycle of the cod worm, a parasite that lowers the value of cod. The bounty on seals was supposed to eradicate the cod worms by short-circuiting their life cycles.

Codfish are a favorite food of harbor seals. When the seal eats the fish they also ingest encysted cod worm parasites. The high body temperature of the warm-blooded seals induces the worms to lay their eggs.

The eggs then pass through the seal's digestive tracts and are broadcast into the oceans with the seal's feces. Snails and crabs eat these eggs and are in turn eaten by codfish thus completing the worms' lifecycle.

I suppose we can draw two conclusions from this, one, that seal bounties are a heavy handed way to eradicate cod worm parasites and two, don't eat raw codfish sashimi since the parasites also survive in the congenial environment of humans warm-blooded stomachs.

The 1972 Marine Mammal Act superseded the bounties. Since then harbor seals and gray seals have started to increase and reappear in areas they haven't been seen in decades — much to the delight of Great White Sharks and the chagrin of fishermen.

Normally animals whose offspring require a great deal of attention are monogamous, because it takes the time and energy of both parents to supply all the nurturing. This is true for many species of birds and is occasionally true of Homo Sapiens. We might also expect seals to be monogamous but they are incorrigibly polygamous.

So, why are seals so polygamous? The easy answer to all such questions of animal behavior is that the animal in question is a compromise. Of course every animal represents a compromise between its anatomy, its behavior and its prior evolution. No animal has completed its evolution. Perhaps Sandy's seal can give us a glimpse of how this works.

Seals belong to the order of Pinnipeds, a group of animals that have made the evolutionary transition from a terrestrial lifestyle to a marine lifestyle. The transition has left them compromised. They are adept and graceful underwater but clumsy and vulnerable on land.

If seals had totally forsaken the land as whales have, this would be adequate, however they have not completed the transition. Like so many other animals they have to return to their previous environment to reproduce.

This means they have to seek out safe isolated islands on which to give birth and copulate. This severe compromise is critical. Although they can spread out and live peacefully off the vast resources of the ocean during most of their lives; during breeding season the males become highly territorial, jealously quarreling over valuable pieces of island real estate.

In most species of Pinnipeds this period of competition has led to the evolution of large competitive males, but it also leads to cute immature animals that seek out interspecific companionship. Sandy must have reminded this seal of its mother who had recently weaned him off her milk. Anyway it had lead to a wonderful day.

# CHAPTER 2
## The Tidepool
### *March 24, 2018*

*Sandworm spawning in tide pool. Sandy Tilton*

> *"As the season changes. Spring seems to come in while the tide is out and winter creeps back with the cold waters of high tide."*
> ~ John and Mildred Teal. Life and Death of a Salt Water Marsh.

It is March 24. Patches of snow still dot the shore of Pavilion Beach, but the sun is struggling to break through the pewter sky. It holds the promise of spring after our long winter of stormy discontent.

I have come out here with Sandy Tilton and Marc La Croix to see how sand makes its way to Crane's Beach. Marc's drone takes off and disappears over Plum Island Sound on its way to Sandy Point.

We lean into the monitor and see acres of shallow sand flats, a long thin sandbar and where 500 feet of new sand has accreted to the end of the point. It is now only a short swim from the shallow water flats of Plum Island to Crane's Beach; but it is an impossible swim, because of the tidal currents that rush through the narrow opening.

Someday, sand flowing off of Plum Island will seal off the mouth of the Parker River and it will have to find a new way to get to the ocean. We can see where that will be. The March storms had smashed through the dunes and undermined one of the Parker River Wildlife Refuge's most beloved boardwalks.

The waves had also come close to forming a new inlet from the ocean into Stage Island Pond. When this does happen, it will make Sandy Point into an island connected to Crane's Beach by walkable sand flats. And Ipswich will gain several hundred new acres of dunes, beaches, uplands and clamflats.

Changes like these have happened out here since the last Ice Age. Then, the ocean level was 200 feet lower and the coast was almost three miles further east. Wooly Mammoth strode across the landscape that we were standing on, which was itself under half a mile of ice.

The glaciers had ground their way through New Hampshire's White Mountains pulverizing their granite cores into millions of tons of quartz, magnetite and garnet sand that the proto Merrimack River had washed onto the Continental Shelf.

As the seas rose they shaped this reserve of Paleolithic sand into barrier beaches and then gently nudged them toward their present locations making what we now call Crane's Beach, Plum Island and Plum Island Sound.

By the time we finished filming it was close to low tide so Sandy and I wandered down Little Neck to see how much the storms had also filled in the Ipswich River.

Sandy knew every nook and cranny and could tell stories about each rock, pebble and dune. Walking with her was like walking with myself, where I had grown up on Cape Cod.

Today she was searching for a heart-shaped rock she had discovered several years before. She knew the location of dozens of heart-shaped rocks and believed Nature had put them there for her enjoyment.

She pointed to a large rock. She and her brother had almost been stranded on it when the tide had caught them unawares only a few years before. She explained that when she was a girl the thing to do was to swim across the mouth of the Ipswich River at slack water, then swim back as quickly as you could before the outgoing tide swept you out to sea.

We lingered at a tidepool that she used to visit with her daughter. It was almost perfectly round, fifteen feet across, and protected by a 4-inch tall wall of peat. The perimeter of the peat was covered with a profusion of periwinkles, preparing to hunt on the incoming tide.

The tide pool was only a few inches deep but it cradled blue mussels, oysters, boat shells and clean white barnacles in an isolated world of red and green algae. It was like looking back into Paleolithic times, because all these plants and animals had evolved millions of years before humans had appeared on our planet, and millions of years before this shore had been created by the rising seas.

Suddenly we noticed an eight-inch long sandworm swimming sinuously on the surface. Its body had a bluish green iridescence flecked with spots of red and gold. It poked its head out of the water making it look like a tiny Loch Ness monster with two sets of intelligent eyes.

It looked up at Sandy and swam in her direction before burying its head in the sand and thrashing its tail. Soon we saw another worm on the other side of the pool doing the same thing.

But this time I noticed that after the worm thrashed its tail the water turned milky and we could see the feathered feet of nearby barnacles kicking something into their mouths. And a gastropod army of predatory mud snails advanced waving their proboscises in the water to pick up the scent of this new source of food. They looked like Hannibal's elephants galloping in for the charge.

Then it hit me these were Nereid worms, <u>Nereis virens</u>, the sea nymphs of the ocean and we had chanced upon their spawning dance. Like Sandy's childhood friends they were taking advantage of the low tide's slack waters. It was the day before the quarter moon when the tidal currents were at their weakest so the sperm would stay in the tidepool and fertilize eggs that the female worms were extruding out of their underwater burrows. In forty-eight hours this pool would be full of tiny drifting trochophore larvae.

If we had wandered by half and hour later we would have missed this annual spring ritual that is triggered by the phase of the moon and the rapidly changing day-length.

But we had allowed Nature to guide our walk and seen this sensual ritual in a sun-warmed pool so similar to where life may have first evolved.

# CHAPTER 3
# On Wigwam Hill
### *March 27, 2018*

*After the storm, Crane's Beach.*

March 27 held the first hint of spring. The sun shown down on a landscape of white snow, gray dunes and dark vegetation. The wind was blowing briskly onshore so I decided to explore the protected dunes behind Crane's Beach.

But first I had to cross over a boardwalk that spanned the brooding waters of a maple swamp. The maples were rooted in the soil of the glacial drumlin under the swamp, and the sun reflecting off the swamp was profoundly black. However, soon its waters would be filled with egg masses of frogs, newts and salamanders and replete with the calls of spring peepers.

Immediately after the swamp, I entered the realm of shifting sand. The face of the dunes were thick with wooly Hudsonia and rimmed with the branches of pitch pines that could thrive in the sterile soil of the dunes.

I had the feeling that coyote were eyeing me from behind the ground hugging pitch pines only twenty feet away and I could see where the paths of deer cut through the carpet of mosslike Hudsonia tomentosa that made the dunes look like the moors of Great Britain.

Soon I was climbing steep sand dunes still harboring snow. In the summer temperatures in the bowls of these parabolic dunes would soar to over a hundred degrees and the wind would wring water out of any unprotected vegetation. This was why any shrubs and trees had to have deep roots to reach down into the drumlin soils or shallow roots to spread out and catch any rainwater percolating through the sand.

Scattered along the path were strips of dried out vegetation that looked like pieces of old shoe leather. When I poured water on these Geaster hydrometricus, Earth Stars, their leathery appendages started to fold down and raise up a proper looking mushroom. Half an hour later the fungus had swollen into a puffball that released millions of spores into the gentle winds.

At the bottom of the dune field I entered a thick forest of pitch pines, their branches weighed down with pine cones filled with seeds. The seeds would provide food for birds and mammals that would then defecate them out as nutrients to build up the soils even further.

I finally climbed to the top of Wigwam Hill. It used to house a village of Agawam Native Americans, then a house built by the owners of the Crane Estate. Here I was surrounded by oak trees covered with translucent galls made by flies that had laid their eggs between the thin tissues of the oak tree leaves. Although they signified disease, the galls didn't seem to have caused undue damage, and they looked like old-fashioned Christmas tree lights against the cobalt blue sky.

Scattered amongst the dunes were what looked like dwarf apple trees. Much of this area had been farmland before it had been covered by the slowly migrating dunes. In the past people had seen apples growing on what looked like four-foot high apple trees. But that was a chimera. As the dunes moved on they revealed that these were just the tops of twenty-foot high trees that had been buried for over fifty years.

I had found the femur of a cow on the beach several years ago. It was all that remained of half a dozens farms that the Trustees of Reservations had demolished when they had been given the land in the 1960's.

This was the reason you never heard about erosion on Crane's Beach. Even though it was eroding just as fast as nearby Plum Island, its buildings had been removed so there was no erosion problem just a naturally eroding barrier beach.

The dunes beyond the Wigwam Hill drumlin were twenty to thirty feet high and covered with the thickest coat of Wooly Hudsonia I had seen in years. But there was one exposed bowl of sand that had the most abstract set of animal tracks imaginable.

At first I thought they were deer tracks deformed by the soft sand, but they were too wide and splayed for deer tracks, perhaps they were from a turkey.

I posted pictures of the tracks on a natural history photography site and found that these professionals were equally perplexed. Some thought they were horseshoe crab tracks, others from aliens, jabberwockies or jackalope. One opined that they were not tracks at all, suggesting rather darkly I thought, that I might have made the tracks myself. I dearly wished I had such skills.

Finally I turned to the source, Paul Rezendez exhaustive reference, *Tracking and the Art of Seeing.* He explained that when a deer walks downhill in soft sand it opens the halves of its front hooves then steps into that track with its closed rear hooves. Since the sand is soft it also picks up the delicate tracings of the deer's dewclaws that are almost an inch above their hooves.

And finally when the doe had pulled her hooves through the deep sand she had left drag marks marking her passage. I must have interrupted her morning saunter only moments before.

It had been a fitting end to my day of early spring exploration.

# CHAPTER 4
# The Birds!
*April 3, 2018*

*Courting Turkeys.*

I have discovered that just when you think you have nature all figured out, she loves to throw you a curveball. April 3 was no exception.

It was another starkly beautiful day. It had snowed the night before and the early morning daylight peeked out from beneath low clouds that threatened rain. But my house in Ipswich was surrounded with new spring arrivals. Red winged blackbirds were establishing nesting territories in the swale of phragmites beside our house and robins were listening with cocked heads for the faint scrapings of earthworms burrowing through the soft spring soil. A pair of red-tailed hawks were engaged in one of their high-flying aerial courtship flights accompanied by screams and calls of wild abandon.

I figured it would be the perfect day to write about the arrival of shorebirds and fish on Crane's Beach. We had past April 1, the official time when piping plover are supposed to start courting and the sandworms were mating, so squid and lobsters couldn't be far behind.

But my first hint that something might be amiss came when I asked the parking lot attendant what the water temperature was off Crane's Beach. It was 41 degrees. But most marine creatures don't really get active until the water temperature tops 50 degrees. That was when horseshoe crabs start mating, alewife start entering herring runs, and striped bass arrive hungry to feed on sand launce, squid, eels and herring.

But the sun had not been able to heat up the mudflats to raise the water temperature enough to cause the overturn of nutrients that make spring underwater almost more dramatic than spring on land. Instead I found the beach unrecognizable.

The March storms had clawed thirty feet of sand off the front of the beach and deposited it in foot deep drifts a hundred feet back into the secondary dunes. The primary dunes had been sheared off as if a giant cheese slicer had cut them off.

I found evidence of three old barns and apple orchards that had been planted in the rich glacial soil in the late 1800's. They included old timbers and the femur I had found a few years ago.

The town fathers had wisely forbade anyone from cutting the pine trees that held the back the dunes but in the 1830's Humphrey Laksman cut them down to fire his blacksmith shop. The dunes started migrating and quickly buried his orchards, farm and rich soil under 20 to 30 feet of sterile sand. Later the dunes would bury the house on Wigwam Hill so that only its solid chimney remained exposed.

For years the top branches of the apple trees stuck above the dunes where they continued to produce big edible apples on what looked like only three-foot high trees.

But the dunes continued to roll over the landscape until 2002 when a storm sheared 50 feet off the face of the dunes revealing the exposed tree trunks of the apple trees that had been buried for over a hundred years. Now the gnarled black branches of this orchard of petrified apple trees sprawled on the sand beside the pounding surf.

But where were the shorebirds? I hadn't seen a single bird, not even a seagull on the beach. But I had seen where dozens of piping plover had padded through the newly washed over sand prospecting for new nesting sites.

Such washover areas are the prime nesting area for this endangered species and now they had almost a hundred acres of potential new nesting sites. But the entire population of nesting adults should have been on the beach by the end of March. Their tracks were there but where were the birds?

I had expected to see scores of plovers feeding at low tide or resting after flying all night, but there were none to be seen. I asked a former plover warden where they might be and he said it was like this every year. The plover had not established their nesting sites yet so they were not territorial. This allowed them to remain together in large flocks and hunker down in the sand where they were almost impossible to see.

So there was probably a large flock of the endangered species hiding on the far end of the beach. Hopefully they would survive this inclement weather and raise a bumper crop of chicks so we could continue to hear their plaintive calls against the backbeat of our ever pounding Atlantic Ocean.

# CHAPTER 5
## Murder on the Marsh;
## Snowy Owls and the Evolution of Migratory Behavior
## Sandy Point
### *April 17, 2018*

*Snowy Owl lunging at a Canada Goose. Pete Gray photo.*

On April 17, I paid a visit to a pioneer in the evolution of migratory behavior. She was a healthy, well fed snowy owl sitting on her usual perch on a high dune overlooking a lagoon on Plum Island's Sandy Point.

Most snowy owls have to hunt both diurnally and nocturnally in order to find enough food to thrive. But this owl had adopted crepuscular behavior, hunting in the low light of both the evening and at dawn. Then she would use her white camouflage, night vision and ability to fly noiselessly to swoop down toward a sleeping duck until it was awoken by the pressure waves coming off the owl's wings.

The duck would jump out of the marsh vertically, then hang stationary for second before righting itself to attain its maximum flying speed, which was several times faster than that of the owl. But the owl would have already lunged directly at the neck of the terrified bird that had never encountered such a formidable predator. With one quick bite of her powerful beak it would be over. Every time I visited the owl I found the decapitated carcass of a duck or goose that were often twice as large and heavy as the rapacious owl. Good thing for us, she is no longer the size of her distant cousins, the Velociraptors.

After eating her full, the owl would return to the top of the dune where she blended in with the white sand and snow, to be unseen and unmolested by coyotes and photographers that she probably thought were equally predatory. A snowy owl in Salisbury had adopted the opposite strategy, showing off and becoming friendly with the photographers who flocked to its perch on top of a light pole every day.

But most of the snowy owls sat in the nearby low marshes only able to squeak out a living by hunting tiny voles, or being sucked into the engines of jets at nearby airports that looked like the owls' featureless flat homelands in the Arctic.

So, how had this pioneer bird discovered that her perch was so superior to those selected by other snowy owls? Did she somehow realize that selecting and defending this territory would provide her enough protein to return to the Arctic to raise her own chicks? Was she just luckier, smarter or more adventurous than other snowy owls?

Scientists have long been as intrigued with the evolution of migration as that mystery of mysteries, the evolution of species themselves. Their fascination was perhaps expressed most memorably in Jurassic Park III when Alan Grant sees the pterosaurs flying out of their electrified enclosures and utters something like, "Good God they really do migrate!"

When scientists first started seriously studying animal migration in the Sixties, they discovered that animals use specific cues like day length, water temperature, and the earth's magnetic field to trigger and steer their migrations. They ended up thinking that animals were like driverless cars that automatically followed GPS to their predetermined destinations.

They also didn't think very much about how such migrations evolved. But the most astute animal behaviorists realized that wasn't really the whole story. Birds blown off course managed to correct their migrations to end up at the correct destinations, not to belabor the analogy, but remarkably like the human occupants of old fashioned driver driven cars!

Other researchers wanted to know why songbirds migrate north when they can just as easily stay in the tropics where food and nesting sites are abundant. Then they discovered that robins that nested in Alaska could successfully raise more chicks that robins that nested in the mid-West because they had several more hours to feed their chicks due to the longer day length in the north. This enabled the Alaskan robins to shave several days off the amount of time their newly hatched chicks would be most vulnerable because they couldn't fly. In the crapshoot that is evolution, such advantages are more than enough to drive birds' migrations farther and farther north.

So today we had an example of the role of intelligence and deci-sion-making in such migratory behavior and it was perched on the dune overlooking the Sandy Point lagoon.

Scientists used to think that snowy owls flew south because of a lack of food. But now they know that snowies actually undertake these irruptions because of an abundance of lemmings, their prime source of nutrition in the Arctic.

Turns out, lemmings are particularly sensitive to global warming which has raised the temperature of the Arctic tundra so high that the rodents can no longer rely on having cold fluffy layers of insulating snow to protect their tunnels and nests. Populations of the voracious rodents also fluctuate because they explode when predators like Arctic foxes move off the tundra, then they collapse after their exploded populations consume all the fields of lichen the lemmings depend on for food.

Many people of a certain age are convinced that when food becomes scarce lemmings commit mass suicide by leaping into the Arctic Ocean. Little do they know that they were conned by the magic of Uncle Walt. When the Disney crews were filming the lemmings for their popular films about the Arctic, they had people off camera flinging the poor creatures into the Arctic for effect.

Be that as it may, during the years when lemmings are abundant the snowy owls can raise three or four chicks rather than their regular one of two, thus doubling the owls' populations. The same thing happens with small geese called brant, but because they have evolved the ability to lay as many as 30 eggs they can increase their population almost thirty fold in a single generation.

But then the nesting pairs chase the immature owls off their feeding territories, so the young birds move off to find new food. But they don't automatically fly south as scientists in the Sixties might have expected. They zig zag back and forth looking for places that have food and look like the Arctic tundra.

But a few particularly perceptive owls find places like high dunes overlooking duck filled lagoons preferable to anything they ever saw in the Arctic. They are the pioneers that could be turning their irruptions into true migrations. If they do, it will be because of a few wise old owls that learned something in their impressionable teenage years.

# CHAPTER 6
## The Great Cranberry Bog Mystery
## Salisbury Beach
### *April 24, 2018*

*State archeologist Victor Mastone inspects mystery tracks in a former cranberry bog.*

In 2004 I wrote an article for the Boston Globe about some wagon tracks and hoof prints that had appeared in the surf after a severe storm on Cape Cod. The tracks looked like they had been laid down the day before, but they had actually been made 300 years ago. Then, Cape Codders used horses and oxen to cut salt marsh hay and ship it to what we now call Hay Market Square in Boston.

The tracks also showed that the beach had migrating 800 feet inland in the intervening 300 years because the sea has risen over three feet since the 1700's.

So when natural history photographer Sandy Tilton sent me photographs of fossilized hoof prints she had taken on Salisbury Beach, I figured I had about the same thing on my hands.

On April 24th we went down to investigate the site with state archeologist Victor Mastone, and we quickly realized Sandy had discovered a much more complicated site.

The biggest difference between the two sites was that the Salisbury hoof prints had been made in clay while the Cape Cod tracks had been made in peat. So the Salisbury prints were a lot more distinct than those on the Cape. Plus there were no tracks left by hay wagons in Salisbury, so this had not been where people had been cutting hay.

Our second thought was that the site might have been a hard spot on the marsh where farmers kept their horses during the haying season. But that didn't explain the other artifacts on the site.

The clay was about a foot thick and stretched along the beach for almost a quarter of a mile. Most of the hoof prints were concentrated in the center of the site but there were also hoof prints and even human footprints concentrated in small areas throughout the site. Then there were ancient scratches in the clay that looked a little like the markings in Nazca Peru that only make sense when you fly over them in a plane.

There were also pieces of metal and wood scattered throughout the site, but the most perplexing artifact of all were a set of small, deep seated parallel tracks that ran in a long straight line.

We tossed around several theories for what had gone on at this site. Perhaps it was the location of a small farm or even where colonialists had salvaged a wreck, but these explanations also had flaws.

The clay was our biggest dilemma. Victor mentioned it had probably lined the bottom of an ancient pond. That night it hit me. You often find stretches of wild cranberries lying in clay-bottomed swales behind the dunes in places like nearby Plum Island and Crane's Beach. They are not like commercial cranberry bogs that you see flooded with several feet of water. The wild bogs grow in only a few inches to a foot of water depending on the season.

A wild cranberry bog would explain why we had only found the roots of mostly a single type of vegetation embedded within the clay. These would have been from the cranberry plants that are only a few inches tall.

So probably Native American Indians and later colonialists harvested this bog for hundreds of years along with horses and ever-advancing cranberry rakes whose wooden tines left scratch marks throughout the bog.

Sandy did some research and discovered that cranberry harvesters used to use double handed rocker scoops that they would sweep back and forth in front of themselves while wading through the shallow bogs. They would take a step, dip the long fingered tines below the plants then rock them back to pluck the berries which would roll back into the scoop. This would have accounted for the short gait of the parallel tracks. These rocker rakes were invented in 1830.

So we can surmise that sometime after that date a group of people had finished harvesting the cranberries in late September, then a series of storms had blown wind off the tops of the nearby dunes, burying the tracks and causing the dunes to migrate and fill in the bog.

The sand from the overlying dunes would have protected the tracks, wood, metal and scrape marks in the slightly compressed clay. Then, the series of storms and high tides we had in 2018 washed away the overlying sand revealing the tracks glistening in the still moist clay for the first time in at least 180 years.

Coastal geologists use a rule of thumb called Bruun's Rule to estimate how far a beach will migrate as the sea rises. According to this rule, for every foot the sea rises, a typical beach will retreat between a hundred and three hundred feet inland. So this beach had retreated between 180 and 440 feet during the past 180 years. Of course this retreat was not uniform. Some years the beach would hardly seem to move at all. Other times it might erode 20 feet in a single storm.

We had an example of such rapid erosion in the dunes just behind us. Two eighteen wheelers were dumping tons of sand on an access point between the dunes and excavators were using it to build berms and shore up dunes in front of houses that the storm had left teetering on the edge. The sand would provide protection for a few short months or perhaps years, but like the cranberry bog in front of them, in less than ten years the inexorably rising seas would wash many of those same houses away with the tides.

# CHAPTER 7
## The Herring Run
## Essex, Massachusetts
### *April 30, 2018*

*Night heron hunting for alewives. Sandy Tilton.*

I decided to celebrate the last day of the worst April in history by joining marine biologist Peter Phippen at the Essex herring run. It was yet another cold, gray day with intermittent rain. The day before hail had been pelting down on our roof.

The cold temperatures seemed to have delayed the run by about two weeks. The fish usually don't enter the runs until the ocean temperatures are between 50 and 54 degrees. But the stream was running fast from all the recent rain.

Ninety percent of these fish were actually alewives; Alosa pseudoharengus and only ten percent were true blue backed herring, Alosa aestivalis. The most important difference between the two is that the alewives spawn in the quiet waters of ponds and lakes while the blue-backs can spawn in the rapidly running streams leading up to the ponds.

The alewives get their nickname from an amateur ichthyologist who noticed that the ten-inch long fish were heavier in front so he thought they looked like the buxom wives of ale serving tavern owners. Now there is an ichthyologist who needs to get out way more often.

We were watching the herring from about halfway up the run. But we weren't the only ones watching. We heard a distinct "kronk, kronk, kronk" call before we spotted three black crowned night herons perched amidst the red buds of maple trees that were overhanging a pool just below the state's solar powered counting station. The heron looked like miniature gray vultures hunched over against the rain.

The herring warden had written down the number of herring that had squeezed through the counting station's wide-winged weir, 1,217 fish yesterday, 19,934 fish since April 1 and 38,000 fish the year before. So we were almost half way through the run, despite the cold rainy weather.

Suddenly we heard a rush of water and saw fins and swirls on the surface, but curiously the herons didn't even twitch. A small school of fish had just made their way up the rushing stream and into the pool where they were milling about as if encouraging each other to finish the final leg of their journey to Chebacco Lake. There, the male alewives would fertilize the eggs as the females extruded them out of their vents onto strands of vegetation sprouting from the bottom.

Many of the herring would be picked off as they passed through the gauntlet of cormorants arrayed along the shore. Those that did reach the lake would remain for a few weeks to lay and fertilize the eggs.

A few of the fish had already accomplished their pleasurable evolutionary task. One was slowly descending the stream. He faced into the current gasping to retrieve what little oxygen the fresh water could hold. He had a large white patch where a seagull had pecked him on the back. The mishap had removed the slime coating that protected him from infection. So a deadly fresh water fungus now infested the spot.

But his odyssey would soon be over. Ocean waters would kill the fungus and the herring would start feeding again. His body would readjust to the increased salinity and he would survive.

Beside him another fish would probably not be so fortunate. It was a fresh water sucker that had been swept down Alewife Brook. He was hugging the bottom between attempts to swim back upstream. But he was a poor swimmer unfit to battle such rushing waters. Each attempt only swept him closer to certain death in the waters below.

Similar incidents must have happened innumerable times in the early development of this area. Runoff from melting glaciers swept numerous fresh water fish into newly forming estuaries — estuaries rich with limitless supplies of plankton and small fish.

The proto herring that were able to survive the gradual change in salinity were amply rewarded. But their eggs could still not survive in salt water. Gradually some fish evolved that could make it back to fresh water ponds to spawn. Obstacles to the success of such migrations were great but the advantages were legion. Over time the herring developed what animal behaviorists call a stable evolutionary strategy, one uniquely adapted to exploiting both the protection of fresh water ponds and the rich abundance of the oceans.

Then, just to prove the researchers wrong, in the 1940's herring ascended the Welland Canal into Lake Michigan and found the area so congenial they gave up their migratory lifestyle. In fact their populations exploded becoming such a threat to larval lake trout that wildlife managers introduced salmon to keep the herring in check, instead the salmon just outcompeted the lake trout for food.

But the herring's new lifestyle had risks. They lacked the large kidneys of fresh water fish that had to keep peeing so that their cells would not become swollen and rupture from the osmotic pressure.

This physiological stress made the Great Lakes herring sensitive to fluctuating water temperatures. So when the herring left the deep waters of the lakes to spawn in the spring, they often encountered upwelling currents which caused the water temperatures to rise so quickly that huge numbers of herring would die, leaving odoriferous piles of the invasive species on the shore. But it was the same species that provided us with such pleasure on a cold spring day in New England.

# CHAPTER 8
# Spring Arrives on Sandy Point!
## Sandy Point
### *May 5, 2018*

*On the way to Sandy Point. Sandy Tilton.*

After a long drawn out winter, spring arrived with a bang in early May. So I decided to visit Sandy Point. The dusty road through the Parker River Wildlife Refuge was lined with scrums of photographers scanning the bushes for migrating warblers.

Most of the photographers had a camera and lens worth over a thousand dollars and some had tripods, camouflage, blinds and lens worth thousands of dollars more. I probably passed close to $100,000 in camera equipment. Hunters spend about the same for guns and ammunition, justification enough for those who need good hard economic reasons for why parks and recreation should be encouraged.

Then a softer justification came by in the shape of a 1910 model T flivver trundling down the road heading for Sandy Point. I was instantly transported back to a more innocent age.

Sandy Point was about 500 feet wider than the summer before. And the shallow water made it look like the Bahama Banks bone fishing flats.

Pure white sand was blowing over the dark moist sand surrounding the lagoon and piling up as miniature sand dunes behind tufts of grass, horseshoe crab shells and even the remains of a duck's egg. The egg had probably been laid by an immature female who hadn't learned to build a nest before just laying her eggs willy nilly on a windswept beach. We had one do the same thing on our recently cut front lawn.

Piping plover were rushing down to the shore then back to their nests behind the symbolic fencing that rangers had erected to keep people away from stepping on the nests that were really just scrapes in the sand.

The rangers had also picked up the worst of the debris left by the March storms, so that now the beach was wide, inviting and already covered with sunbathers. Boaters would start arriving in earnest after Memorial Day.

I decided to walk around the point where clammers were busy turning over the clamflats in pursuit of soft-shelled clams. The bluff behind the beach had taken a beating. Trees slanted out at odd angles, but this provided an arboreal lesson simple enough for even a lowly science writer to understand. I usually separated my trees into tall leafy trees, short leafy trees and conifers.

But along this shore each tree was decorated with its own distinct blossoms. Of course even a writer can recognize a pussy willow. Their puffy white buds had already matured in to two-inch long catkins attracting hordes of pollinating insects.

The second most plentiful trees were black cherries with 5-inch long clusters of round white petals. But the trees' most distinguishing feature was their dark gray bark covered with perfectly etched out scales.

These wild cherries had evolved a clever strategy for their dispersal. Birds, mice, foxes and coyotes loved to eat their edible fruit but couldn't digest the pits so they would poop them out along the edges of fields and in dunes. Wild mice also helped the cause by hoarding the seeds in empty birds' nests and in their underground burrows.

The blossoms of the yellow birch were the most difficult ones to recognize. Their long green catkins would produce small brown cones chock full of tiny wind driven seeds. The birches had grown up reaching for the light above the shell and dirt road that used to lead to a beautiful old seaside cottage on the Ipswich bluffs side of lower Plum Island.

The remains of the recently demolished home reminded me of the four hermits and one widow who used to live on Plum Island Sound. But that could be explored at another time. Now it was just pleasant to snooze in the warm welcoming sun!

# CHAPTER 9
## Three Hermits and A Widow
## Plum Island Sound
### *May 5, 2018*

*Hermit House?*

In 1962, an autumn storm shipwrecked Jack Helfant's houseboat on Sandy Point. Rather than making his way back home he simply decided to stay on the island using driftwood, canvas and parts of his houseboat to make a shack that he covered with salt hay. Later he added another room, which he called his parlor.

That first summer, Jack was not well received by the hundred or so other boaters who lived in a tent city overlooking Ipswich Bay. They complained to the Ipswich Board of Selectmen who dispatched the town's health officer to scope out the situation.

The inspector found Jack clean-shaven and no sanitation problems. Besides, the tent owners had grown to like Jack and convinced the selectmen to just let him alone. This was convenient because in

Massachusetts you can't evict anyone who hasn't established residency and by law that would take twenty years, a nice little Catch 22 for the veteran of 19 years in the service.

Over the years Jack made more friends and he and his pet collie Prince became permanent fixtures of the island. Teenaged boys would bring Jack supplies or ferry him to the Pavilion Beach store to buy things like batteries, which he purchased with money from his veteran's pension.

But the one thing Jack didn't like was to be called a hermit. He was just a man who enjoyed living alone, communing with nature and enjoying his own thoughts.

Lewis Kilborn was born on Lime Street in Newburyport, but when he was a week old his parents took him to Grape Island in the Plum Island marshes. He was educated in the Grape Island School, which only held classes in the summer. The town paid his teacher to teach and live on the island in the summer then move back to the mainland to teach again in the winter.

Lewis completed the 6th grade before learning the fishing and clamming trades. Before long he had his own fishing boat and set his lobster traps from the Isle of Shoals to Boston Harbor.

He also took care of his father until the old man's death in 1946. During that time Lew would write up a list of supplies he needed and give it to his friends to purchase the items on the mainland.

Lew endured several hard winters on the island, particularly the memorable Blizzard of '78 when snow drifted over his roof and covered his windows.

During such emergencies Lew would raise a white flag over his house and the Ipswich shellfish warden would drive down to the Ipswich Yacht Club, flash his lights and blow his horn four times so Lew would know to take his boat across the Sound to pick up his emergency supplies.

Lew never left Grape Island. When his friends and family tried to convince him to leave, he demurred saying the mainland was just too damn crowded and that he was more than happy living with nature and the wild animals that became his pets.

In 1984, Lew's nephew Jack Dolan was bringing supplies to his uncle and found him collapsed beside the chair where he used to smoke a corncob pipe and regale his friends with stories of the island that he had lived on for over 80 years.

Lew was the last resident to live on Grape Island. After he died his house was razed and the island returned to its natural state. Lew would have liked it that way.

Bill Marble was a free spirit if not a hermit. He used to live in Georgetown in winter and in his Plum Island camp in the warmer months, where he fished for a living and raced boats on Kenoza Lake in Haverhill in his early years.

The Great Atlantic Hurricane of 1944 caught Bill unawares on Plum Island because he lacked a radio or newspapers to warn him of the storm's late September arrival. The storm destroyed Bill's boat, along with the Vineyard Sound Lightship, two Coast Guard cutters and the USS Warrington with 248 men aboard.

Bill was marooned for three days because the twelve-mile hike to the Coast Guard station was too far for a man in his Seventies to handle. So he had just hunkered down and ridden out the storm, spending many more summers on the island only dying in 1953.

Bill's friends gathered on Bar Head and buried his ashes under a large boulder Bill had chosen for his tombstone that had the name of his favorite poem "Outward Bound" etched into its side.

Even though the beach changes drastically every year Bill's boulder remains in its place near the entrance to the Bar Head trail. Sometimes it is covered with debris from winter storms other times it is clearly visible above the shifting sands.

The fourth hermit who lived on Plum Island Sound will not be identified for obvious reasons. Like the others she preferred to think of herself more as a widow than a hermit. After her husband died she just remained in their camp making a living harvesting cranberries, and catching flounders and shellfish.

One night she was awoken by the voices of four men inside her kitchen. She reached under the wooden bunk for her husband's old shotgun and said, "Who's down there? What's going on?"

"Don't you worry lady. You have nothing to fear. You just stay upstairs and we'll make it right for you."

She couldn't make out any more words but figured there had to be at least 3 or 4 men, a boat and a truck parked beside her camp. She huddled back under the blankets and waited until the house was quiet before venturing downstairs. There on the edge of her kitchen table was a crisp hundred-dollar bill.

"Now wasn't that nice of those kind gentlemen. Next time they come I think I'll make them some piping hot cranberry muffins."

It was said that the mutually beneficial business arrangement continued for many profitable years.

# CHAPTER 10
# Right Whales and A Wronged Swan
# Gloucester, Massachusetts
*May 10, 2018*

*Swan mating or attacking?*

In early May I heard rumors that Right Whales were feeding off Gloucester's Eastern Shore. I thought my chances of seeing the whales were slim, but how many times do you get to see endangered species swimming just offshore?

If I saw what were supposed to be four or five whales I would be seeing one percent of all the North Atlantic Right Whales in the world and five percent of the hundred individuals in New England. It certainly seemed worth a try.

Brant were dabbling in the quiet waters beside the Eastern Point breakwater that protects Gloucester Harbor where a tall schooner was sailing toward the horizon and fishing boats were steaming toward their fishing grounds.

A group of engaging kids from East Boston were on an Audubon sponsored marine biology field trip. They told me they had just seen whales swimming north, so I decided to drive along the shore until I found a spot where I might be able to see them.

This entailed driving around a beautiful old ice pond where several cars had pulled over to watch a pair of swans mating beside the road.

The male was standing on top of the female holding her neck in his beak as animals often do to get leverage doing coitus. But we quickly realized something was seriously wrong. The male was repeatedly slamming the female's head onto the ground. He wasn't making love he was trying to kill the female in the most horrific manner possible. She was already scared, exhausted, wounded, and near to death.

It was clear that this battle had started in the pond where the male had been trying to hold the female's head underwater while using his superior weight to drown her.

By this time two other people realized we were witnessing a murder so we did our best to keep the male off the exhausted female. This was dangerous because a full-grown swan can break a man's arm with its powerful wings. But the male was so intent on getting back to the injured female he ignored us.

After several tries we were finally able to herd the male into the pond where he arched his back and rose up out of the water flapping his wings in what was an obvious victory dance that would have got him ejected from any NFL football game.

Feathers strewn along the shore revealed that this beating had been going on for almost an hour and would have continued even longer if we hadn't intervened. The female's head and back were bleeding from where the male had been repeatedly bludgeoning her and apparently he had broken her leg because she couldn't walk.

By this time other cars had stopped and we were able to piece together the actual story. The male was called "Pappy" or simply "Mr. Swan." He had lived on the pond for over 28 years, but last year a coyote had killed his lifetime mate.

What we had assumed was a female was actually "Tos" a year old male who had been raised from an egg by some nearby residents who had introduced him into the pond as the ice was breaking up. Everything had worked out just fine until "Pappy" had returned and spent the last two weeks trying to drown what he thought was his younger rival.

We had just witnessed what happens when a species has not evolved a means to stop aggression during a battle to establish dominance. Animals that have sharp claws or teeth that can instantly kill a member of their own species have also evolved releaser mechanisms to stop aggression once dominance has been established. The classic example of such behavior is when two dogs fight. As soon as one dog rolls on his back in a display of submission it is impossible for the dominant dog to continue fighting, often displacing his aggression by biting at the air.

Unfortunately animals that we usually think of as being pacific lack such a positive morality because they lack instantly lethal weapons, so if their enemy can't get away a swan or dove will spend hours gruesomely pecking it to death.

The same is somewhat true for humans. As soon as an opponent says "Uncle" we know we should stop fighting. Spectators want to see their team dominate another team or establish say, that Boston is clearly dominant over New York, but despite what they say, spectators don't really want to see one person brutally bludgeon another to death.

The problem with humans of course is that we have learned how to build artificial weapons but have not had the time to evolve the morality of a wolf.

It was gratifying to see that as soon as we realized what was happening we dropped our cameras and ran to assist "Tos" who was eventually rescued by some animal rehabilitators who released him in the ocean far away from the homicidal "Mr. Swan."

Not far away I found the Right Whales cavorting just beyond some large plutons of orange colored granite. They made the shore look like Northern Maine. The whales were diving, spouting and filtering the surface with their large open baleen plated mouths fishing for copepods, herring and mackerel.

A long smelly sheen of fish oil lay on the surface, which had attracted several flocks of voracious seagulls. Waves exploding against the granite cliffs carried the smell of the oily excrescences directly to my nose.

But there was something strange going on. There seemed to be several pods of whales with three or four individuals in each pod. I could see dorsal fins as well as smooth-backed whales. Later I found out that the fins were from Sei whales that often feed with Right Whales.

After half an hour a fishing boat came cruising along its regular track and also started to fish. Boats are not supposed to come within 500 yards of an endangered Right Whale but in this case it was the whales that were actually approaching within 50 feet of the boat. After satisfying their curiosity the whales backed off and continued feeding. The men were so preoccupied with their own fishing they didn't even turn around.

This was the reason there are so few of this magnificent species left on our planet. These were the "right" whales to catch because they hugged the shore, were easy to approach and they floated after they had been killed.

It is said that there used to be so many Right Whales between Boston and Provincetown that a man could jump from one back to another to cross Cape Cod Bay dry-shod. Now there are less than a hundred individuals left in New England waters. None of them had calved this past year and I had been privileged to see one percent of all these leviathans left on our planet in a single afternoon.

# CHAPTER 11
# Horseshoe Crabs
# The Life You Save May Be Your Own
### *May 15, 2018*

*Encrusted horseshoe crab. Sandy Tilton photo.*

It is May 15. The new moon hangs in the late night sky. There are no sounds save for the quiet lapping of waves against the shore. The beach awaits the high tide, the highest of the month. There is an expectant sense of creation in the warm night air for it was in shallow waters like these where life first evolved.

Offshore, a male horseshoe crab has just reenacted a ritual that has survived for over 400 Million years, long before there were birds, fish and dinosaurs on our planet. When the first horseshoe crabs crawled ashore to lay their eggs the only thing on land were mosses, ferns and a few dragonflies with three-foot long wingspans.

But this male crab is in trouble, his exertions during spawning flipped him over and now he is trying to arch his back so he can use his tail to right himself. But he is top heavy from an encrustation of barnacles, mussels and even a European oyster attached to his shell.

He is using valuable energy to flip himself over. If he doesn't, at sunrise seagulls will find the crab and tear out his fragile book gills. This will allow Gram-negative bacteria to surge into his blood system. Gram-negative bacteria are as fatal as they sound and are ubiquitous in shallow waters like those in Plum Island Sound.

However, the crabs have a primitive but elegant defense against Gram-negative bacteria. Unlike humans that have over 26 different types of cells that make up their immune system, horseshoe crabs only have a single type of amoebocyte cell. The cells simply migrate to a wound and coagulate to keep the infection out of the crab's blood system.

Humans are also susceptible to Gram-negative bacteria that can cause often fatal diseases like spinal meningitis, Gonorrhea and toxic shock syndrome. In the Seventies Dr. Frederik Bang at the Marine Biological Lab in Woods Hole discovered that the blue copper based blood of horseshoe crabs could be used to make Limulus amoebocyte lysate or LAL to test for the endotoxins released by these Gram-negative bacteria.

Whenever anything comes in contact with the human blood system whether it be a syringe, vaccine or artificial knee, it has to be tested for Gram-negative bacteria and the way that is done is with the LAL test.

So, today this processed horseshoe crab blood is worth over $30,00 a quart, and several large pharmaceutical companies produce LAL and sell it worldwide.

All this lysate is being made from a single species of wild animal, and as you would expect, that animal is declining up and down the East Coast, breaking a link in the chain of life that includes several species of endangered shorebirds like Red Knots, who time their migrations to and from Tierra del Fuego to the Arctic so they will be on Delaware Bay in May to consume up to 40 tons of horseshoe crab eggs. This will allow them to lay their own eggs as soon as they arrive on their Arctic nesting grounds.

Theoretically the decline in horseshoe crabs should not have happened because crabs are supposed to be bled for LAL then released back into the wild with no mortality. But under industrial conditions, things inevitably go wrong and the crabs often die from transportation or being overbled, which sometimes kills up to 50% of the crabs.

But things might be starting to change for the crabs. In 1997 Dr. Jeak Ling Ding at the National University in Singapore filed a patent to use recombinant technology to produce a synthetic substitute for LAL.

However the FDA refused to regulate the substitute because it wasn't a blood product and wasn't used to diagnose or treat a disease so they claimed it was out of their jurisdiction.

It wasn't until 2012 that the FDA came around and announced that pharmaceutical companies could use the substitute LAL but they added a kicker. The companies had to prove that the artificial LAL worked better for each drug they produced, so there was little incentive for them to do so, since LAL continued to work just fine and the companies were already familiar with how to use it.

It was not until 2017 that Lee Bolton, a researcher at Eli Lilly who also happened to be a birder, convinced the company to use the substitute LAL to test the water they used to make pharmaceuticals in a new plant they were opening in China.

Then on May10, 2018 he held a press conference at the New Jersey Audubon Center to announce that Eli Lilly planned to start using the synthetic substitute to test the water it used in all its plants in the United States. This would reduce Eli Lilly's use of LAL by 90%.

If other companies follow suit it could save the lives of half a million crabs and they would return to only being used as bait for conchs and eels which is a much easier problem to solve because it turns out fishermen are much more amenable to change than pharmaceutical companies. Who would have guessed?

# CHAPTER 12
# Terns and Plover; Crane's Beach
## *May 22, 2018*

*Jeff Danancourt repairs fence to keep predators out of the tern colony.*

In mid-May Jeff Danancourt from the Trustees asked if I wanted to join his team of ecologists putting up solarized fencing around four new acres of washover area on Crane's Beach.

The first thing I noticed was how productive the washover area was. It was crisscrossed with footprints of blackbirds, plover and least terns that had paused to feed around tussocks of wrack and debris. Some of the tussocks had scape marks where the plover had started to make their nests. But there were also tracks of crows, foxes and coyotes, searching for plover eggs. They had plundered two of about forty nests the ecologists had already identified.

The electric fencing was designed to keep such terrestrial predators at bay but at least one coyote had learned that he could jump over the fence and back again with an egg in his mouth.

Least terns were returning from just offshore with silversides held crosswise in their bills. A male landed and presented the silversides to his coquettish mate. Apparently the silversides convinced the female that the male would be a good provider so she accepted his offer to mate. It was important that she chose well because both adults would have to fish fulltime in order to raise their chicks. Young adults often had trouble rearing any chicks and more experienced adults could only catch enough food to raise two or three chicks if silversides and sand launce were not abundant that year.

Of course the electric fence couldn't stop avian predators. Jeff explained that in past years he had built large enclosures both around and over some of the nests.

But such an exclusionary device just looked like big food courts to Great Horned owls. They had discovered that if they landed on top of an enclosure and flapped their wings a petrified plover would scoot out the bottom and the owl would have his supper. It reminded me of a high school friend who discovered that if he kicked our school's vending machine in just the right spot a bottle of coke would come trundling down the shoot.

Jeff explained that wildlife managers were in what amounted to an arms race. Every year he would try something new to thwart predators, but by the end of the season the predators would have learned new behaviors to circumvent his strategies. So this year Jeff had decided to not put up any exclusionary devices at all.

But erecting the electric fencing was a little like putting up Christmas tree lights. If the wires on one of the panels were broken the entire system wouldn't work so we had to check for power in each panel until we found the defective wire and then repair it with a simple sheep's bend knot.

Blades of dunegrass could also bleed electricity out of the system reducing the voltage from about seven volts near the power source to less than two volts on the far side. But this was still enough juice to give a coyote pause. Finally Jeff set a timer he had jury rigged into the system so it would only be activated from 8pm to 8am.

By the end of the day I was reminded that Crane's is one of the best-managed beaches in New England. Every day thousands of beach goers share the beach with hundreds of pairs of nesting terns and plover. The trustees also don't allow beach buggies on the beach so there are no conflicts with human beach goers and endangered shorebirds.

I mentioned to Jeff that one of my pet peeves was that when most of the environmental laws were promulgated in the Seventies, scientists and politicians decided to put the emphasis on protecting endangered species rather than protecting habitat. I have often felt protecting habitats would be more effective and avoid the animosity aimed at innocent species like plover and spotted owls.

But Jeff pointed out that Crane's Beach also provides a perfect example of how protecting a species can also protect the environment. The symbolic fencing not only protects the birds but it also allows rhizomes of dunegrass to quickly expand into washover areas to help build up new dunes.

I also noticed that the dunegrass was much healthier here than on Plum Island. Part of the reason was the presence of the plover that spent all day feeding on grubs, ants and sand fleas that lived in the wrackline of the overwash areas.

One of the reason you see die-off areas on Plum Island is that the dunegrass has been attacked by fungus and nematode worms. It seems possible that the plover also eat the tiny nematodes, thus protecting the dunegrass.

# CHAPTER 13
# Breaking New Ground
# The Hillside Center
### *May 30, 2018*

*One of the Hillside Center's well insulated homes.*

On May 30 I visited the Hillside Center for Sustainable Living. When it starts renting its one, two and three bedroom homes, scheduled for late fall, it will be the first urban, agriculture focused, solar powered community in the country.

The Center is the brainchild of David Hall who developed and owns the Tannery. As an undergraduate David studied zoology at the University of New Hampshire and became immersed in the environmental movement.

So it was natural that he wanted to use his development skills to build a community that would target the three largest emitters of global warming carbon dioxide; housing, food and transportation. The Newburyport community will accomplish these goals through having a 420 KW solar array that will provide more energy than the center needs so it will sell its excess electricity back to the national grid.

The Center's homes will be so well insulated that they will only need the equivalent of a blow dryer to heat them even on cold winter nights, and the center's fruits and vegetables will be grown in the edible landscaping throughout the campus and in a 1500 square foot greenhouse.

The solar canopies over the site's two parking lots will be used to power electric vehicles available to the residents for downtown shopping. Residents will also be able to take short walks downtown or catch a train to Boston at the nearby Newburyport train station.

Hall used innovative resources from the start. First he found an inexpensive brownfields site where the city's coal ash had been buried at the Hiller farm. Then he was able to win a $400,000 grant from the state to remove the affected soil.

Finally, he obtained permission to salvage 2.5 million pounds of large granite blocks from the demolition of the Whittier Bridge. These are being used for building foundations and for a retaining wall whose risers and steps will be planted with plants and edible vegetation.

Rainwater will be harvested from the rooftops of all the buildings and stored in a 100,000-gallon cistern underneath the greenhouse. The water will then be piped throughout the center to irrigate agricultural areas, wash laundry and flush toilets.

Visitors will enter the Center through the year-round greenhouse and step into a spacious common area that will include a commercial kitchen so farmers can add value to their produce and so food can be prepared for occasional meals and other group activities. Guests can also be put up in rooms above the common area. Affordable housing units will be available through a partnership with the neighboring YWCA.

The most interesting aspect of this project is that it is a for profit venture that will have to make money to succeed. I have visited similar projects run by non-profit groups that have access to grants, foundations and tuitions that give them more leeway to succeed or fail.

If the Hillside Center can succeed in the profit-making marketplace, it could become a model for similar sustainable communities in other parts of the world.

# CHAPTER 14
## Castle Hill
### *May 4, 2018*

*The remains of the Crane's swimming pool and casino for entertaining.*

The best way to understand the early history of Castle Hill is to go to the south side of the Crane Estate's Great House where a plaque embedded in the wall replicates the deal made between John Winthrop Jr. for the town of Ipswich and Masconnomet, for the Agawam native Americans. Masconnomet sold "Castle Hill and all the surrounding meadows and marshe" for a rifle and twenty pounds of clamshells, wampum being the coin of the realm for trade between settlers and Native Americans in 1634.

Not a bad deal for Winthrop who had told the town he would build a fort on the hill to defend Ipswich, but moved to Connecticut to become Governor there instead. The Winthrop family was a bit like the modern day Bushes, having governors in almost twenty percent of the 13 original colonies.

Since Native American culture didn't recognize that land could be owned, it is unclear whether poor Masconnomet really understood that he had just given Agawam land away in perpetuity. He was undoubtedly dispirited at the time. Ninety percent of his people had died in the plagues of the white man's diseases that decimated Native Americans from 1616 to 1619. They had left behind their already cleared land and laboriously built dugout canoes, called water horses by the settlers who then used them in their creeks and marshes.

But the curious thing was that the settlers were already referring to the area as Castle Hill way before anything like a castle was even on the hill. It is possible a few of the remaining Agawam had built a palisaded fort on top of the hill but some think that the prophetic name came by way of Captain John Smith who wrote about the castellated hills on a fair "Isle of two or three Leagues, covered with "many cornfields and delightful groues."

The most recent purchaser of the land definitely had a castle on his mind when he bought the land from John Burnham Brown in 1909 for $125,000. It was the last time the multi-million dollar peninsula would be conveyed for cold hard cash.

The buyer was Richard Teller Crane a young Chicago industrialist who made toilets for a living. He had previously studied philosophy at Yale and it is doubtful he ever contemplated running the small foundry started by his hard driven father.

But when Richard's older brother resigned as head of the firm, Richard had taken over, later stating that his ambition was "to make America want a better bathroom," even though the Crane Corporation was into all kinds of other things including building elevators and making valves and fittings for Naval vessels during the First World War.

But the fundament of the business sat on plumbing, which graced such grand venues as Chicago's Drake Hotel and the thrones of King Hussein's Hedjaz palace in Mecca. Who says water and oil don't mix?

Richard was always known as an unpretentious and endearing man, but his wife Florence was a bit high maintenance. When the young couple first visited the North Shore, Florence wanted to build a summer cottage to match her social ambitions in tony Manchester-by-the Sea, but Richard had fallen in love with the fair "meadows and marshe" of Castle Neck.

So Richard commissioned Shepley, Rutan and Coolidge to design a 60 room Italianate castle, but Florence found it cold and drafty. So Richard made her a deal, if she didn't grow to love the house after ten years he promised to tear it down and build her another. She didn't and he did, hiring the Chicago architect David Adler to design a 59 room Stuart style county manor. I guess it was time to downsize,

In order to help the landscapers Richard bought in an innovative new steam shovel he christened "Cyrus" even though his workers were known to refer to it more often as "The Florence H".

New Englanders have always looked a little askance at the goings on of the wealthy people who came to relax on their shores in the summer. At the same time they are also a little of proud of their very own celebrities and titillated by their extravagant ways.

The Cranes arrived every summer in their own Pullman car, which remained on the rural town's sidings until the Cranes returned to Chicago at the end of the season. They lived at the end of Argilla Road, which presented something of a cultural dilemma.

The rest of the road was peopled by what were called the MGH mafia; Boston based doctors and surgeons who preferred to live as simple farmers and fishermen in the summer. One North Shore socialite described Argilla Road as being "inhabited by queer people whose children go about barefoot and wear bloomers".

So imagine what it must have been like for the Crane's children closeted up in the castle having to dress up for dinner while their friends ran barefoot through the dunes. But it must have been a respite from their even more restricted lives in Chicago, because both Florence and Cornelius became fast friends with their more bohemian neighbors, Sarah Crockett and Sidney Shurcliff whose father had designed the Great House's surrounding landscaping.

# CHAPTER 15
# Phased Retreat; The Nauset Strategy
# Orleans, MA
*May 25, 2018*

*The Nauset Beach Administration building will be moved to an adjacent motel bought by the town in anticipation of sea level rise.*

I'm fortunate in that I grew up in Orleans, a town with twice as much coastline as that of New Hampshire, in fact our Congressman used to boast that his district had more shoreline than any other district in the country. So on May 25 I decided to return to see how my old stomping grounds had fared during the preceding March storms.

Not well. Nauset Beach's beloved Liam's Clam shack, renowned for it's non-pareil onion rings, had been undermined by waves and demolished. The old-fashioned bandstand had washed away and 80 feet of dunes had been lost allowing waves to slam up against the large old administration building and the town had removed a row of parking spaces so they could build a new barrier dune.

These changes had not been unexpected. In fact the town had proactively purchased the parking lot of a vacant motel on a hill several thousand feet back and above the existing lot.

They had also hired the Woods Hole Group to prepare a detailed analysis of the dynamics of the beach, which it turns out had been off by two years. They had stated forthrightly that storms and erosion had accelerated because of climate change and sea level rise from about two feet per year from 1868 to 1994, to over 12 feet from 1994 to 2015. Using that present rate of erosion they had predicted that Nauset's beach infrastructure would be inundated by 2020 not 2018, which just proves that weather is always a rogue.

But it didn't really matter. The town had implemented its phased retreat so that excess parking and administration activities had already been moved to the higher location. Plus, a row of parking had been sacrificed in order to create an attractive outside eating area serviced by five food trucks. People were already grousing that Tex-Mex could never replace the redolence of Liam's sweet smelling fried onion rings, though local cardiologists figured one was just as good as the other for their trade.

I was proud of my town for accepting that our increased erosion was being exacerbated by sea level rise and had acted decisively to carry out a strategic retreat, much like Washington during the Revolution, Grant during the Civil War and the Brits at Dunkirk, which had made D-Day possible.

The Woods Hole Group has designed a similar plan for Crane's Beach and the state has hired them to analyze the cost effectiveness of purchasing a dredge, which will be a boon for North Shore communities.

It would certainly make sense for Newbury and Newburyport to hire the group to devise a similar comprehensive plan to create enough parking, on and off site, to serve Plum Island while at the same time earning enough revenue to fund the lifeguards and bathing facilities paid for by the communities fifty years before.

# CHAPTER 16
## One Good Tern Deserves a Plover
## Crane's Beach
### *June 12, 2018*

*Newly hatched plover peeking out from beneath his mother.*

On June 12 I returned to Crane's Beach to check on the nesting shorebirds. I had first visited in late May. It was the first hot weekend of the season, and by 10 am the parking lot was already half full. People were happily setting up beach chairs, breaking out food and starting to build large elaborate sand castles.

I decided to cut through the dunes, which were ablaze with the bright yellow blossoms of heath-like Hudsonia tomentosa. When I returned to the beach I saw the changes in the nesting area.

There were fewer adult plovers sitting on nests but lots of long-legged chicks searching through the wrackline for food. Because plovers don't feed their chicks after they hatch, the young birds are mobile and can start feeding themselves as precocious little hatchlings.

I walked a mile up the beach to see how my favorite pair of plover were doing.  Four weeks before the female had been sitting on four eggs and she would stalk out boldly to challenge me.

It was obvious this was an extremely competent mother. Usually plover just scrape a depression on the open beach, but she had made her nest behind a twisted stick that provided cover and camouflage. But her nest was also the closest one to the water. During a recent storm, waves had come within two feet of her eggs.

But today, even though I was only about 6 feet from the nest she didn't move a muscle. She was going to sit on her eggs come hell, high water or intrusive photographers. Occasionally she would chirp at her feckless mate. Eventually he got the picture and did a poor imitation of dragging a broken wing.

She was so bold and competent and he was so drab and ineffectual I had started calling them Sonny and Cher. Besides, who couldn't remember Cher riding her bicycle down the path from the Crane Estate in The Witches of Eastwick?

 After a few minutes I saw why the female had been so steadfast. A tiny head poked out from one side of the nest, then another from the opposite side. The two took a few wobbly steps then ducked back under their mother's feathery breast. But the first chick had what looked like the residue of egg white on her bill. It was likely the chick had been hatching as I had been taking photographs of her mother.

The hatching had occurred just in time. We were still near the peak of the 30-year proxigean tidal cycle so the highest tides of the year would be approaching in two days. But by then the chicks would be able to move up the beach to avoid being washed away. Their mother was not only competent, bold and clever; perhaps she even knew her tides, which were critical to her entire lifestyle as well.

But it was the least terns that caught my undivided attention. I was used to taking photos of common terns that would dive bomb the top of your head, so I had learned to stick a feather in my hat so they would peck at it rather than at me.

But least terns had the disconcerting habit of flying straight for you at eyeball level then stalling in front of your face and squirting a stream of well-aimed guano onto your clothes and camera lens. A pair of oystercatchers flying over the tern colony got the same treatment. A flying mob of screeching terns drove them quickly away.

The same thing happened when the Trustees' ecologists picked their way through the colony counting eggs and chicks. The entire colony of adult terns flocked over to defend their nesting territory.

But the good news was that the ecologists had counted 42 active plover nests with chicks and more than a hundred tern nests, and seen very few signs of predation. All their work had paid off, now the terns just had to make it through the proxigean tides and continue to catch enough sand eels to feed their chicks. They were fortunate to have selected such a congenial place to nest.

In neighboring Gloucester not far away, owners had encouraged their dogs to invade restricted areas to kill off the flightless plover chicks. It was indicative of an anti-environmental backlash that was being fostered by the highest office in our land, and here we were in a country once known for its robust conservation ethic, a sad situation indeed.

# CHAPTER 17
# A Pygmy Sperm Whale in the Ipswich River?
# Steep Hill
*June 12, 2018*

*Dead whale being hauled off the beach.*

Residents of Little Neck received an early morning shock on June 12. A nine-foot long creature was thrashing around in the shoals of the Ipswich River. The creature seemed to be disoriented by the currents and rapidly falling tide. Soon it beached on a shoal and boaters started splashing it with water, thinking they were saving a shark.

Sandy Tilton was asleep on Steep Hill when she saw first Jeff Danancourt, the Trustees' head ecologist, then an Ipswich police officer hustling down the beach at about 4 pm. She went back to sleep until her curiosity finally got the better of her and she walked down the beach to see what all the fuss was about.

Jeff explained that a pygmy sperm whale had just beached itself on the trustees' Steep Hill Beach and the New England Aquarium and the Seacoast Marine Mammal Rescue unit were on their way.

Jeff had spent all day being bombarded by terns. All he wanted to do was to go home, take a long hot shower, and get rid of the layers of guano the terns had squirted at him for the past eight hours. The last thing he needed was a dead whale rotting on his beach. Whales' internal organs have a disconcerting habit of decomposing rapidly, which builds up gases that can explode sending smelly, rotting whale entrails all over people, animals and beaches.

The whale was a strange looking creature. It was almost ten feet long and looked suspiciously "girthy" as if she could be pregnant. Except for her tail she did look more like a shark or even a land animal than a whale. She had a tiny jaw with about nine perfectly formed incisors, but it was her prominent eye that caught Sandy's attention. It was a deep dark bluish green that looked old, wise and infinitely sad, from where the trail of a single teardrop had trickled down her cheek.

Staring into the whale's eye was like looking back in time. Millions of years ago her ancestors had started developing features like large lungs, echolocation and spermaceti organs that added resonance to the clicks they used to sense the location and motion of giant squid. These creatures were precursors to today's regular sized sperm whales.

But their lifestyles were stressful and required tremendous amounts of energy, besides there were lots of smaller squid to be had closer to the surface. Over time nature selected for smaller and smaller sperm whales with smaller lungs and smaller spermaceti organs.

So now, instead of making deep, energy consuming dives and having epic underwater battles with giant squid, pygmy sperm whales can simply laze around on the surface then stop swimming and sink to a depth where they can catch enough small squid to met their modest needs. But it was their habit of floating passively on the surface that made them so susceptible to being hit by passing boats.

By the time I arrived the recovery had devolved into a keystone cops kind of affair. About a dozen rescuers in bright green shirts had rolled the whale onto a orange sling and now it was being hauled up the beach like the carcass of a dead bull being hauled out of the ring by an all terrain vehicle, not a magnificent endangered species. The undignified operation had already obliterated the whale's eyes and abraded her skin.

Reddish brown fluid was oozing out of the whale's vent that made it look like she may have aborted her fetus. Later I discovered that pygmy sperm whales are the only cetaceans that shoot such fluid out of their vents to confuse their enemies, so like the squid that constitute their main prey item.

Everything has to go just right for a whale to successfully give birth. Time is of the essence and the baby has to be born tail first or it will drown. Then the mother has to help it to the surface to get its first breath. If there is a breached birth and the baby comes out headfirst it will drown before it gets that all-important first breathe.

I wanted to suggest that someone reach a gloved hand into the vent and feel around for a tail, better yet someone should have done that when the female was still in the water, to see if her calf could have been saved.

But by this time it was clear that the ATV wasn't strong enough to drag the whale to where it could be loaded onto a truck and rescuers were making plans to tie the whale to a tree so it wouldn't wash away during the night and making phone calls to their superiors about how to handle the press.

Someone finally had the presence of mind to take the Ipswich police up on their offer to tow the whale by boat to the town landing where it was loaded onto a truck and taken to a special facility in Quincy for a necropsy to find out why the whale died.

On June 23 the New England Aquarium released the results of their preliminary autopsy. They found that the whale had been pregnant with a half-term fetus even though it had been late in the calving season. Plus, they found about 200 squid beaks so she had been eating normally.

But they also found <u>Crassicauda magna</u> a parasitic roundworm that can grow to be nine feet long and had laid eggs. The roundworms are only found in pygmy sperm whales, and they often wrap around a whale's head and could have interfered with our whale's ability to get out of the rapidly falling waters of the Ipswich River.

# CHAPTER 18
# Horseshoe Crabs and Clammers
# Sandy Point
### *June 24, 2018*

*Mating horseshoe crabs on Sandy Point. Sandy Tilton photo.*

June 24 was a warm, sultry summer day. The afternoon sun glinted off the tightly packed cottages that dotted Great Neck and two tall wind turbines spun in the onshore breeze. The full moon would be in four days and we were still in the proxigean tides so several dozen clammers were bending over their rakes taking advantage of the extreme low water.

It was not difficult to imagine what these flats looked like 500 years ago. Great Neck would have been covered with a scattering of long houses surrounding fields the Agawam kept open through yearly burning and kept fertilized by alewives from the nearby Ipswich River. By June the fields would already be covered with subtle green clusters of corn, squash and beans, the three sister crops that had sustained their ancestors for untold generations.

The clammers would have been mostly women then, bantering back and forth as they dug clams with sticks and loaded them into long dugout canoes instead of into today's aluminum skiffs.

The thing you wouldn't have heard were clammers complaining about the "F'ing" horseshoe crabs. I felt like I was back in the Fifties on Cape Cod after the state had declared horseshoe crabs shellfish predators and encouraged Cape Cod kids to turn in horseshoe crab tails for a two-cent bounty.

We even had a Labrador retriever who had picked up the habit by watching us catch the crabs. Jake would spend all day wading in the shallow waters until he felt a crab with his paw, then he would plunge his head down below the surface, grab the crab by the tail and haul it up the beach.

When the crab righted itself and started to crawl, Jake would dig a hole in front of the hapless creature and wait for it to tumble in. Then Jake would bury the crab and return to the water to search for more crabs. He taught three generations of dogs to catch horseshoe crabs, but by the third generation they would just haul the crabs up the beach and bark at them all day long.

But now we know that horseshoe crabs feed primarily on worms, detritus and tiny Gemma gemma clams that look like quarter inch quahogs but are actually full-sized adults. More significantly we now know that if you keep a horseshoe crab in the wild and only bleed it once a year for biomedical purposes, it is worth over $3,000 over its lifetime. So today's shellfishermen were killing an animal worth $3,000 to protect an animal worth only a few bucks a pound.

But some of the old timers never got the memo and continued to impale horseshoe crabs on their rakes, spilling out the crabs' cobalt blue blood that is worth $30,000 a quart when it is used to test for often fatal bacterial diseases like spinal meningitis and toxic shock syndrome.

Such random killing has had a negative impact on both the crabs and the endangered shorebirds that feed on their eggs. But the last time anyone did any kind of systematic count of horseshoe crabs in Plum Island Sound was in 1952. That was when Carl Schuster measuring the width of horseshoe crabs in estuaries from Maine to Florida.

On July 27 1952 he caught and measured over a thousand adult horseshoe crabs in Plum Island Sound in the morning and about the same number in the afternoon.

He discovered that horseshoe crabs are largest and most plentiful in Delaware Bay and get smaller and less plentiful as you go both north and south. He also discovered that Plum Island Sound has the smallest horseshoe crabs of any estuary on the East Coast because of fresh water from the Merrimack and Parker rivers and our cool northern waters. Today you would be hard put to catch 50 crabs let alone 2,000 behind Plum Island Sound in one day. But if the existing crabs are not killed their populations could bounce back quickly because each female lays about 4,000 eggs a day for four days on both the new and full moon high tides.

What we need are accurate counts of both the breeding adults and their immature offspring. This can be done in both the spring when the adults are spawning, and in the fall when the immature have cast off their empty shells.

Both are perfect exercises for citizen scientists. In the spring the volunteers can count the number of male and female crabs mating in a designated section of beach. In the fall, volunteers can count the number of shells cast off by immature crabs along a 50-foot section of the wrackline. Their numbers could range from less than a dozen crabs shells for an unsustainable breeding population to several hundred shells for a healthy population.

Several volunteer groups are planning to work with the state to get these numbers and to initiate a program to collect horseshoe crab eggs and raise them in tanks until they are large enough to ward off predators.

After horseshoe crabs reach about an inch across they have few predators but as eggs and part of the plankton they are like tiny little ice cream cones. Birds, fish and mammals all like to eat them. It will be interesting to see whether this exercise will have enough impact on Plum Island Sound's natural population of crabs to appear in the data collected in the potential spring and fall crab surveys.

# Chapter 19
## Choate Island Stories
### *June 23, 2018*

*The Choate House.*

Don Paquin's family has been intertwined with the Crane family for two generations. His father worked for the Trustees at the Crane Estate for 28 years, Don for almost as long. One day, early on in their employ, Don was due to meet Mine Crane who was arriving for the season and Don told his father that he was nervous because he had never met her before. But his father insisted he had.

"You remember when you broke your leg when you were six years old?"

"How could I forget?"

"Well Cornelius was in the same hospital because he was dying and his wife Mine, this beautiful woman from Japan would visit him every night. Well one night she asked us if it would be alright if she came in to sit with you as well."

"So for 54 days she would come into my room and sing these beautiful lullabies. Now part of my present job is to take care of Mine and Cornelius' grave on top of Choate Island. It feels like I'm returning her kindness to me from when I was just a young kid."

Don told the story on a boat tour through the five islands and marshlands that make up the Crane Wildlife Refuge. He is a born raconteur and an invaluable asset to the Trustees that own the Crane properties.

The cruises came about after the Trustees bought an aluminum float boat to ferry contractors to Choate Island so they could build a 17th century Potemkin Village for *The Crucible* that starred Winona Ryder.

"But before we had even bought the boat Elizabeth Choate called and said, 'Now Donnie I understand you are planning to give tours of Choate Island. That is just wonderful but I think members of the Choate family should be on that first cruise.'"

"I explained that we still didn't know exactly when the cruises would start but to keep in touch. So for the next four years she would call every week and say, 'You know Robert who lives in Missouri, he would love to come on your first cruise along with George's family from Kentucky. You remember George don't you'? Of course I had never met any of them in my entire life.'"

The tours started a few years later but when Don told his passengers that they would be going to Hog Island to see the Choate House, Elizabeth stood up in the stern and said crossly,

"Now Donnie I'm very mad at you!"

"What for?"

"You just said we would be going to Hog Island to see the Choate House. We will be going to Choate Island to visit the Choate House!"

"Several years later I read in the obituaries that Elizabeth had died and I told one of the members of her family that it was too bad that she hadn't lived long enough to see the name of the island changed to Choate Island."

"Oh she did. The day before she died she got the letter from the US Board of Geographical Names. She died the next morning. I think she just hung on until she received that letter."

The Crane's were much beloved in Ipswich where they supported all the local charities and even established the Cable Hospital after one of Richard Crane's guests died from a heart attack because they were too far from the nearest hospital. The family also set up a fund so that every year all the kids in the Ipswich schools take the day off and go to the beach on Cornelius Crane's birthday. Mr. Crane tried to start a YMCA in Ipswich but the old Yankee town fathers turned him down and Ipswichites had to wait 75 long years to finally get one.

But the most beloved member of the family was Mine. She loved to stand in the field and paint pictures of the deer that lived on Long Island. So one year Don's predecessor Walter Prisby mowed the grass in the big field on the island so that it read, "Welcome Mine" when she returned from Chicago.

Mine loved it so much that the following year Wally drove to Russell's Orchards and asked if he could buy a bushel of apples that had been crushed up to make apple cider. Then, every week he would buy another bushel and spread them out in the field and toot his horn to get the deer's attention.

When she arrived Wally told Mine that he had been talking to the deer and they said they all wanted to greet her when she got back.

"What do you mean you talk to them?"

"Oh yes, we have long conversations. They are very smart. Come on out I'll show you."

When they arrived at the big field one or two deer were waiting but Wally was upset.

"They told me that all of them would be here. Now where could they be? Oh I forgot, they said to toot the horn when we arrived."

So Wally blew the horn and several hundred deer galloped out of the woods to welcome Mine back to the beloved Crane Estate her family had bequeathed to The Trustees.

# CHAPTER 20
# St. Peter's Fiesta Gloucester
*July 1, 2018*

*St Peter's Fiesta!*

"Viva, viva, San Piehhh…tro!" The deep voice bounced off the high walls on either side of the narrow street leading down to St. Peter's Square. It was followed by ten guardians dressed entirely in white carrying the statue of the mother of grace down to where Saint Peter's statue waited for the outdoor mass to begin.

"Buon Giorno" intoned a handsome young priest and a thousand voices answered "buon giorno" from behind programs being used as temporary fans to ward off the heat and humidity of the hot summer day.

The priest was followed by Gloucester's formidable Mayor Sefatia Romeo Thekan who started to read, stopped, looked at the beginning of her notes, then looked at the end of her notes, then out at the audience and said, "I cant read this. It's in Portuguese!" Had she been pranked by the Portuguese half of her city who shares Gloucester's rich fishing heritage with their Sicilian compatriots?

This is the St. Peter's Festival that has been celebrated in Gloucester for ninety-one years. Similar festivals have been celebrated for hundreds of years on Sicily where fishermen started to walk out on a greasy pole that juts out from a vertical cliff above the Mediterranean.

And it celebrates Peter who was a young fisherman like these Gloucestermen who were about to try to walk out on their own greasy pole to grab a flag and swim back to shore, and become a local heroes for the rest of their lives.

But Peter was fishing in Lake Gennesaret in what we now call Syria when Jesus told him to lower his net "whereupon it filled with a huge number of fish". What fisherman wouldn't be impressed with such a miracle? So Peter became Christ's first disciple.

But fishermen can also be skeptical cusses. Three times Peter denied that Christ was the Messiah until finally at the last supper, Jesus chided him "Oh ye of little faith, why did you deny me?"

But Jesus must have seen something in the young fisherman for he gave him the keys to the kingdom of heaven and told him he was "Petros", the rock, on which his church would be founded. And thus did this simple young man become the patron saint of fishermen, the bishop of both Rome and Antioch and the first pope of the Catholic Church. Not bad for a fisher of men.

But the significance of the festival goes even further back than those two thousand years. We live on a planet that is blessed with productive oceans and land, but the oceans have no higher plants and lots of fish and the land has no animal protein to speak of but lots of vegetation.

It is only when fishermen catch fish and transfer them to the land that we and our planet flourish. The Paleo Indians knew this when they used alewives to fertilize the soil for their staple crops; corn, beans and squash.

And it was only when Paleolithic people lived beside productive estuaries that they had enough food to support permanent year-round settlements, without having to rely on the irrigation, agriculture, taxation, bureaucracy, separate classes and slavery that are the basis of our what we now call our modern civilization.

I wonder if we are really happier than when we were simple fishermen and farmers living as equals beside each other in an Edenic world? But those are just the thoughts of a backsliding Unitarian. "Viva San Pietro!"

# CHAPTER 21
## Greenheads and Tides
## Crane's Beach
### *July 10, 2018*

*The daytime high tide was about a foot lower than the nighttime high tide because of the declination of the moon.*

On July 10 I walked 200 feet into the marsh near Crane's Beach to test my theory that you can use the Proxigean tides, often called king tides, to predict flooding events. In this case the event would be the drowning of this year's crop of greenhead flies. These vicious Tabanids have ruined many a day at the beach. Last year one bit me on the lip, which swelled up to the size of a grape so I looked like a prizefighter all day.

The immature flies live in the high marsh as inch long transparent larvae that creep through the wet thatch until they encounter prey, which is usually one of their own kind. The larva then sneaks up on his brother and impales him on a syringe like proboscis. The two flail around for several seconds until the victor sucks all the bodily fluids out of his equally cannibalistic brother.

By the beginning of July the larvae start emerging from their pupae as adults that fly straight to the nearest beach for a nice dinner of human blood. This will provide them the protein they need to lay their eggs back in the sweet gray mud of their natal marsh.

Their lifespan is usually cut short when the first full or new moon high tide of August drown the larval pupae before they can hatch. But this year the proxigean tides would be falling in mid-July, an extremely rare event, and my hypothesis was that the tides would shorten the greenhead season by almost a month to the delight of beachgoers everywhere.

My theory seemed to be panning out. I walked the length of a 200 foot dock and back with nary a bite. Normally I would be covered with itchy often bleeding welts. But something was mysterious. It was high tide but the incoming water wasn't covering the upper marsh.

When I returned home I checked the tide chart and found my answer. The night high tide had been a full foot higher than the day high tide. This is because the moon was orbiting the earth at about 22 degrees above the equator. It wobbles up and down across the equator throughout the year. It is only when the moon is directly opposite the equator that the day and night tides are equal.

So I had learned that the proxigean tides can predict events like the drowning of greenhead tides but could they also predict when people's homes were at risk of being washed away? That would be the big enchilada.

In 1978 Fergus J. Wood correlated several hundred years of erosion events with the proxigean tides and discovered a significant congruence. Today environmentalists are using king tides to show what the coasts will look like as the seas rise. But there is a problem. We are still near the peak of the proxigean tides that have a 30-year cycle.

So sea level will appear to be dropping for the next 15 years and journalists will stop writing about it until about 2045 when the seas will be over a foot higher — add that to twenty foot waves, twelve foot tides and five foot storm surges and you have a real problem. But writers will have moved on to other stories that have more immediate news pegs.

If you don't believe this, look at articles from 30 years ago when both Time and Newsweek and several other periodicals like Scientific American had major stories about sea level rise. But they were actually writing about the effects of the proxigean tides that were at their last peak 30 years ago. As Friedrich Hegel wrote, "The only thing we learn from history is that we learn nothing from history."

# CHAPTER 22
## Time and Tide
## Sandy Point
### *July 15, 2018*

*Time and tide. The lowest tide of the year. Sandy Point.*

---

*"The exposed rocks had looked rich with life under the lowering tide, but they were more than that. They were ferocious with life, there was an exuberant fierceness in the littoral here, a vital competition for Life."*
~ John Steinbeck, The Log from the Sea of Cortez

---

The lowest tide of the year fell on July 15, the last of the proxigean tides. The sun glimmered faintly off a moonscape of newly exposed intertidal areas made purplish gray by their fine mix of silica, magnetite and garnet sands.

Craters, eddies, swirls and swales marked the rapid passage of last night's currents over the heavily corrugated sand flats. Myriads of gurgling streams drained pools down to the water's edge where young terns clamored for their parents to bring them ever more wriggling silversides. The young fledglings were already larger than their hard working parents.

The tide was so low it had exposed ghostly tangles of lobster pots festooned with fishing line and lures. I wanted to walk out to far edge of the sandbar where it squeezed up against the distant Ipswich River.

As I started out the sand oozed pleasantly up between my toes. But I soon realized I would have to keep moving or sink into this slurry of water saturated sand. I jumped from what looked like one dry hump of sand to another, but suddenly the entire area liquefied under me and I sank up to my knees almost losing my camera in the process.

I didn't want to get caught in a pit of quicksand as the tide came rushing back in. But I soon discovered that if I walked on the drier, whiter sand of the sandbar I could avoid sinking into another quagmire.

The high tide had spilled over the sandbar last night, leaving behind huge sand murals of phantasmagorical creatures. A standing angel held her twenty-foot wings folded elegantly overhead, a sixty foot long purple squid slithered tentacles first out of the limpid lagoon.

It was as if the moon had reached down an invisible brush and painted the images with long feathery brushstrokes from its palette of silica, magnetite and garnet sand. Tonight's high tide would erase the images and replace them with yet more examples of nature's intricate works of art.

The week before, many of the tidepools held lion's mane jellyfish that had been blown here by an offshore storm. Their pink and red bells were a foot across and they pulsed weakly in the trapped water of the pools. But these stinging cnidaria share the record for the longest animal on earth. Their bells can grow to be 8 feet across and they can trail over two hundred feet of tentacles that make them almost twice as long as a measly blue whale.

The tentacles are covered with stinging nematocyst cells that inject deadly nerve toxins into their prey. When you get stung it feels like you have just swum into a warm patch of effervescent water, then the pain sets in. In 1864, over a hundred people were stung by the tentacles of a single dead but still viable lion's mane jellyfish in nearby Rye New Hampshire.

So far, the clam flats lay beyond the reach of the ever encroaching sandbar. The extreme high tide had separated this intertidal area into several broad zones. The upper zone was littered appropriately enough with <u>Littorina littorea</u> periwinkles.

Two weeks before the tiny gastropods had covered the blades of marsh grass with their masses of transparent egg capsules. The snails had spawned during the weak neap tides so their larvae would not be swept into the predator rich waters of the sound.

The next zone was covered with the shells of steamed clams. This was where shellfishermen dug for them during normal low tides. But seaward of that zone was yet another zone that was only exposed during these extreme low tides. It was emitting a shivaree of squirts and gurgles from thousands of clam holes that were usually underwater so shellfishermen hadn't dig for them.

Beyond the zone of fortunate clams was the world of the tide itself. Sand shrimp lay in the shallows and rice grain sized crustacea that looked like tiny white lobsters careened off my feet every time I took a step. They seemed like they could be an abundant source of food for migrating shorebirds. I had a hunch what the mystery amphipods were but I would have to return with a fine mesh net to make a positive identification.

# CHAPTER 23
## Peeps, Plover and Mud Shrimp
## Sandy Point
### *July 15, 2018*

*Peeps... Semipalmated plover. Steven Liffmann.*

Toward the end of the day I spotted a pair of what my birder friends call "peeps" pecking in the soft mud of the clam flats on Sandy Point. Peeps are particularly difficult to differentiate for someone trained in marine biology. At first I assumed they were just another pair of endangered piping plover, but something wasn't quite right. The looked like piping plover, but their behavior was all wrong.

Instead of chasing after their precocious chicks the pair were standing side by side dipping into the shallow water rather than feeding in the wrackline. Could this be a pair of their far more successful cousins Charadrius semipalmatus, the semipalmated plover?

The only way for a novice to get a positive identification is to check their tracks. Piping plover footprints look like outstretched hands, but semipalmated plover's toes are slightly webbed, making their footprints semipalmated.

Semipalmated plover are also smarter than their cousins. Instead of laying their eggs on exposed beaches where dogs, people and beach buggies can maim and kill them, they nest on the Arctic tundra where only scientists are around to bother them. Consequently, semipalmated plover are the most successful species of shorebirds in the world while their cousins, the piping plover, are just hanging on.

In late July up to 700,000 semipalmated plover fly down from the Arctic and land weak and emaciated on the expansive tidal flats of the Bay of Fundy. Everyday 160 billion tons of water flow in and out of the funnel shaped bay. That is more than the combined flow of all the fresh water rivers in the world.

The bay's tides are over fifty feet high and when they go out they leave miles of exposed mud flats pockmarked with the burrows of billions of rice grain sized mud shrimp that look like the tiny white lobsters I saw on Sandy Point.

Each plover spends 12 hours a day following the tides several miles down the bay and back consuming 7,000 Corophium mud shrimp before taking a siesta and feasting all over again. After two weeks of such gluttonous ecstasy the plovers are plump and ready to make their non-stop flight to the Suriname coast of South America.

Scientists only discovered this crucial stop over area in 1985 when a high course tide forced several hundred plover into the road where they were run over by a car. A pair of graduate students took advantage of the tragedy by slitting open the plovers' bellies and discovering that they were chock-full of the protein rich amphipods.

It turns out our pair of Sandy Point birds had stolen a march on their semipalmated brothers. They had flown down two weeks early and discovered this other stopover area with a source of protein far richer than what their brethren will find when they arrive on the sandy shores of Crane's Beach.

Our mud shrimp were feeding on microscopic diatoms that coated the mud with a fuzz of green. But not for long. Just before the tide came in the diatoms dove into the mud and the flats returned to their normal gray color.

Scientists have recently discovered that the diatoms have an internal clock that keeps track of the tides so they know when to commute back to the surface for their high tide feeding time. Their biological clock is necessary because there are no other reliable clues to warn them when the tide is about to come in or go out.

And the mud shrimp don't just become active when the water covers them as you might expect. They also possess an internal clock that tells them when the tide is about to advance so they can feed or recede, hunkering down in their burrows until the water returns twenty-four and a half hours later. If they didn't have such a precise clock they could never survive the harsh tidal conditions of the Bay of Fundy.

But our old friend the horseshoe crab does them one better. It can keep time over an entire year under offshore sediments where there is no light or temperature changes to trigger their migration back to the shore to spawn on exactly the highest tides of May and June.

Humans also have biological clocks, just not as good as those of mud shrimp or diatoms. If you put a man in an isolation tank with no light or sounds he will we go totally bonkers in 24 hours, a female perhaps a few minutes longer.

# CHAPTER 24
# Too Many Details!
# Plum Island
### *July 18, 2018*

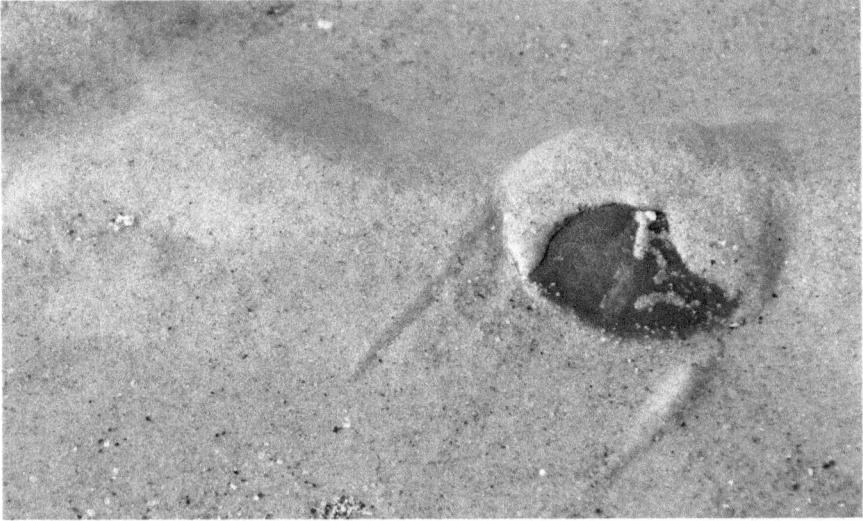

*Sand dollar creeping through the moist sand. Sandy Tilton photo.*

July 18 was a warm sunny day, a blessed relief from several days of heavy rain. So I decided to take a reconnaissance trip to the southern end of Plum Island where I watched sand dollars creeping almost imperceptibly through the moist sand, then went body surfing in the cool refreshing waters.

About two the next morning I woke up with severe stomach cramps and the room seemed to be lurching to the side as if it were in a cabin on the sinking Titanic.

I staggered into the bathroom where I vomited and had severe diarrhea. I became so dehydrated my heart rate plummeted to forty beats per minute and was so weak my wife had to help me get back into bed. I probably should have gone to the emergency room but I opted to sip a bottle of Gator Aid to replenish my electrolytes and go back to sleep.

While I was getting sick, some of the bacteria had backed up into my vestibular system, so I continued to be bilious and dizzy for several weeks.

After I recovered I tried to determine where I had picked up the bug. I had an eye exam a few days before getting sick. Had I picked up a nosocomial bacteria from a medical worker who had not washed his hands? That was unlikely since my appointment had been six days before the event.

The night before I got sick several people in my yoga class had been complaining about gassiness from eating cherries but none of them had come down with the flu.

That left my day at the beach. I checked back and sure enough, I had been swimming after a minor rain event and a severe one a few days before. The rain events had overwhelmed the sewage treatment plants of several small cities causing them to release untreated sewage along with storm water directly into the Merrimack River. From there the sewage had washed down the eight mile long length of Plum Island including along beaches in Newburyport, Newbury, in the Parker River Wildlife Refuge and on Sandy Point State Park.

Hundreds of people had been swimming on those beaches on July 18 but none of the beaches had signs warning people of the danger of swimming or eating clams from the polluted waters.

Over the next month citizen scientists put together what had happened. Only two of the five upstream cities had informed their neighboring downstream communities of the combined sewer overflows in a timely manner. The EPA had an electronic sonde device that measures water quality below the Lawrenceville dam and the health departments in coastal communities are required to take E-Coli counts on a weekly basis and after significant rain events. These were posted on a state website but it is not advertised nor is it particularly timely or user friendly.

The bottom line is that either intentionally or unintentionally the public was never informed of these significant public health hazards that lead to thousands of people being exposed to a toxic soup of pathogens.

Ideally all the beaches along the Merrimack River, and in Newburyport, Newbury, and the Parker River Wildlife Refuge and in the Sandy point state park should have been posted for at least three days after such combined sewage overflows.

In 2015 a peer reviewed health study found a statistically significantly number of emergency room visits for gastrointestinal disorders in area hospitals after such major rain events. So I called the Anna Jacques Hospital and a spokesperson told me the hospital was not notified of CSO events so they could be prepared. Nor would she give me statistics for the emergency room admissions they had after the seven or eight CSO incidents we had, or would have, in 2018.

It seemed like protecting the health of its citizens should be the bare minimum of what federal, state and local governments and hospitals should do. But it turned out that this was just the tip of the iceberg. More events would occur as the long hot summer progressed.

# CHAPTER 25
# Gray or Green?
# Plum Island
*July 22, 2018*

*Art Currier planting dunegrass on the Northern Reservation Terrace berm.*

On July 22 one of Boston's public radio stations, WBUR, presented a well-crafted story about fighting erosion on Plum Island. It pointed out that residents on either end of the developed part of the island had adopted diametrically opposite strategies to achieve similar ends.

The piece opened with Vern Ellis and two dozen volunteers and Reservation Terrace neighbors digging 10,000 holes to plant 20,000 clumps of dunegrass. The roots of the grass would grow 3 or 4 feet into the sand to hopefully anchor the recently built berm in place during the winter's upcoming storms.

Their efforts were a continuation of work that the University of New Hampshire's Gregg Moore had started after he obtained a "Sandy Grant" to help make communities more resilient to erosion. This was what coastal engineers refer to as "green infrastructure", working with nature not against it, to slow erosion.

But a mile up the beach Bob Connors and his neighbors were using a dramatically different approach. In 2012 a March storm washed away six houses and left 29 others uninhabitable for several months. Bob, who sits on the board of The Pacific Legal Foundation, the oldest and most powerful anti-environmental organization in the United States, advised the organization to sue Massachusetts if it continued to uphold its environmental regulations. They called and half an hour later, then Governor Duval Patrick backed down.

The state agreed to look the other way as Connors used his private construction firm's excavators to help build a half-mile long, multi-million dollar seawall that immediately started undermining the beach, and jeopardizing neighboring homes so that their owners were forced to add expensive additions to the already massive wall.

The seawall has failed every year since 2012, costing each homeowner more than $10,000 to repair every year. The wall is now worth almost more than some of the houses it was meant to defend.

Connors tried to make the point that the wall is protecting the marsh behind the dune, which sounded good but was a sham. The seawall will only prevent the beach from moving and re-growing in response to future storms, which is the barrier beach's way of protecting the marsh.

His is the "gray infrastructure" approach that has repeatedly been shown to increase erosion, undermine public beaches and scour out adjacent properties.

But the biggest difference between Bob and Vern is their view of the future. After Vern watched eight tides wash under his house during a single storm in March 2018, he threw in the towel. He now plans to sell his house, not because it might wash away but because it will become harder and harder to sell at a reasonable price.

In contrast, Bob isn't going anywhere and argues that it is the neighborhoods that stand together that will be able to force the government to back down in the face of public pressure.

But what he is asking is that people on both ends of the island acquiesce to his vision of the future — a future of jetties, groins and seawalls, roped off beaches, never ending legal battles against the state and expensive repairs to a multi-million dollar seawall that fails every year to the tune of hundreds of thousands of dollars.

Compare this to the minimal cost of adding a few more inches of sand and replanting the berm every fall and spring. On land that is what we simply call maintenance.

# CHAPTER 26
## You Give me a Straw? I'll Put You in Jail!
## Plum Island
### *July 25, 2018*

*Seagull that was slowly choked to death by a plastic ring.*

July 25 was yet another hot humid day with thick gray fog, greenheads and the risk of thunderstorms. The bobolinks had already departed for the pampas of South America, replaced by large flocks of brilliant white, black and yellow goldfinches busily plucking at the down of thistle heads.

It was a reminder that summer was galloping along and if I wanted to get an underwater look at the creeks and marshes, I'd better get cracking. Besides, my favorite review of one of my books said, "Sargent sees best when his head is underwater". I think it was a commentary on my knowledge of birds and admittedly has merit.

But the strange weather conditions were caused by the jet stream, which normally wanders aimlessly around the Canadian Provinces at this time of year. But this year it had decided to plunge south to entrain the warm humid air over the Gulf of Mexico and convey it north where it had spawned tornadoes in Iowa, tennis ball sized hail in Kentucky, and heat, humidity, flash flooding and rain — torrential rain up and down the entire East Coast.

The greenheads made it uninviting to swim and there wasn't another soul on the beach. In fact the day had a spooky post-apocalyptic feel. The last time New England's yearly climate was like this, the polar caps had disappeared, the oceans were a hundred feet higher and dinosaurs wandered along these shores. Humans have a lot of work and very little time if we want to avoid another Cretaceous age.

But we were in the summer doldrums and I figured I wasn't going to find anything to write about until I spotted the carcass of a dead seagull. It had slowly choked to death, asphyxiated by a plastic tag that said, rather ironically, "Allergy Alert".

I didn't really want to post such a depressing photo but a site set up to discuss erosion control was off on one of its well meaning but time consuming tangents.

The owner of the Beachcoma restaurant on Plum Island was being congratulated for voluntarily replacing plastic straws with biodegradable alternatives. He was winning justifiable plaudits all around.

But his announcement was followed by a "straw vote" to see if people supported having Newburyport's City Council pass a law requiring that the owners of all the other restaurants and bars in the city also provide biodegradable straws.

Opponents quickly posted counter articles about a similar law in Santa Barbara, whose punishment for non-compliant restaurant owners was to throw them in jail and fine them a thousand dollars for each illegal straw.

I hate to say this, but it seemed like the last straw. The city was trying to coalesce around a broad-based plan to make the city more sustainable and to help slow global warming and they wanted to focus on putting people in jail for handing out straws? If we really want to avoid having our planet return to the Cretaceous we don't have time for such nuisance regulations.

I really didn't want to write about the issue, but finally it hit me. This was exactly the kind of environmental regulation that had created the Trump phenomenon, which had caught journalists by surprise to their everlasting shame.

Most of his supporters live off the land and others live close to it. They care as much as anyone about the environment but they have become sick of regulations passed by well-intentioned city lawmakers that negatively affect the lives of people who live closer to the land and have legitimate concerns.

These are exactly the people you want on your side when you tackle issues that we can all agree on, like storms, erosion and sea level rise. If you have ticked off someone about straws, or not being able to repair a dune to protect your house because the dune might have a few sprigs of needle grass, then you are not going to have them as allies when you discuss something like erosion policy, or building offshore wind farms to slow global warming.

# CHAPTER 27
# The Great Monarch Adventure
# Seabrook, NH
*July 20, 2018*

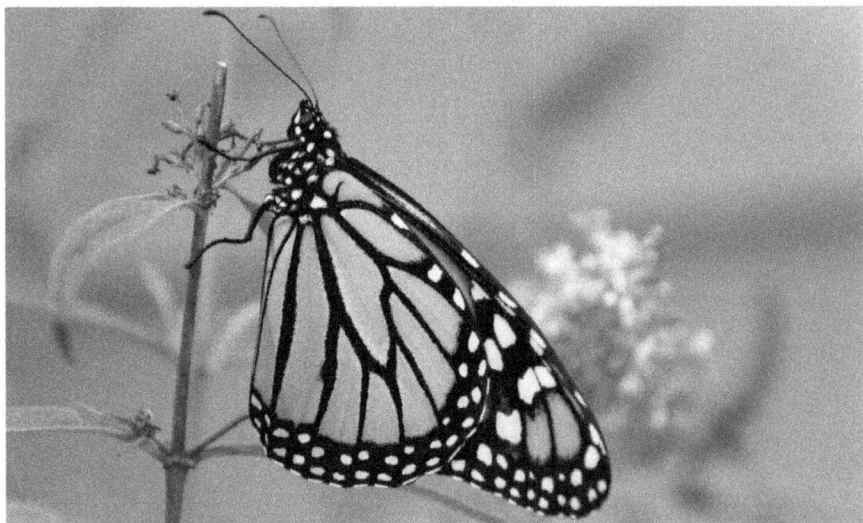

*Newly hatched Monach butterfly. Sandy Tilton photo.*

On July 20 nature photographer Sandy Tilton embarked on an unforeseen adventure. Here are her field notes as posted on the pages of the Plum Island Outdoors Facebook page:

*It all started with a gift of some baby milkweed plants brought for my garden from a field of wildflowers in western Massachusetts.*

**22 July 2018.**
*When I went to water the plants Sunday afternoon I noticed small holes in some of the leaves. I looked a bit closer and 'Ta Da' teeny tiny caterpillars. I started jumping for joy. Me, and my old high school friend Dawn Espinola who had brought me the plants kept finding more and more caterpillars and eggs as well. Yikes!*

*It was a good thing we had been too busy with our school reunion to plant the milkweed, so the plants were still in their box and the caterpillars were safe in my screened in porch.*

**23 July 2018.**
*Dawn and I keep finding more caterpillars and I realize the plants Dawn gave me aren't going to last too long so I have to see if I can find some fresh milkweed leaves.*

*Luckily I find some milkweed close to home and put the leaves in floral tubes to keep them fresh. We find 6 or 7 more caterpillars in the evening. I'm hooked! And off I go to find more milkweed!*

**24 July 2018.**
*Our count is now 8 caterpillars. I call a scientist who raises Monarchs and she advises me to get an enclosure, otherwise the caterpillars will crawl up to the ceiling of my porch when they are ready to start transforming. That will mean caterpillar poop ... everywhere!*

*I find a small cage-like basket and manage to corral the entire little family into the enclosure along with their milkweed leaves. The enclosure allows the poop to fall down through the bottom so the caterpillars don't get infected with germs.*

*I have been reading up on what caterpillars do and what I need to do for them. I have no milkweed field nearby to release them in and I would hate to think of birds getting to them, so I will try to give it my best shot and release them on Plum Island. Will see how it goes. Wish me luck!*

**25 July 2018.**
*Wednesday morning I find one more tiny caterpillar coming out of its egg. I can just barely see its stripes. This is amazing. I put him in the enclosure and hope for the best. Then it is off to the milkweed store!*

Now, every time I drive somewhere I catch myself scanning the roadside to see if I can spot milkweed plants growing where I can easily get to them without getting too many ticks or poison ivy. I might not know where my car keys are but I know where every patch of milkweed is between Salisbury and Plum Island.

**27 July 2018.**
The caterpillars are thriving. I go to the milkweed store every day now and pick twice as many leaves as before.

The caterpillars are all different sizes from my tiny little newbie to the getting really fat guys. One of the mid-sized caterpillars has started hanging from the top of the enclosure and is not eating. Another one seems to be getting orangey colored stripes. Hmm are changes coming?

An old friend posts that Sandy is like the Pied Piper. "Whenever she starts telling a story kids gather like magic."

I guess I was never at a loss for words, when it was story time around the campfire with the kids, or at a bar either for that matter!

**29 July 2018.**
The hanging guy starts to weave a trail of black silk along the top of the cage that is attached to his body as well. He keeps hanging upside down, dangling above the milkweed. I will probably have a #1 chrysalis by morning. This is amazing I gotta tell you!

I subsequently found out that the black silk is actually the caterpillar's skin that it sheds and then eats to fuel its metamorphosis. I'm just as glad I missed that episode. LOL!

**31 July 2018.**
I have the first chrysalis! And two other guys are now hanging from the enclosure. Whenever they come close, they start jabbing at each other, like fighting siblings. Then they stop and begin rocking back and forth in

*perfect synchrony. I can't help wondering what they are communicating to each other. Perhaps it is just from all the pheromones as they prepare to pupate.*

*I can see where caterpillar #1 has made his silk button and before I have to leave for work I have 2 chrysalises. Plus, I find 2 more caterpillars in the box with the baby plants. I still haven't had time to plant them. No time, I have caterpillar chores to attend to. Gotta get back to the milkweed store!*

**1 August 2018.**
*Two more guys are hanging on the top of the enclosure near the #2 chrysalis. One has made his silk button and has assumed the "J" position. I will probably have three chrysalises in the morning! It is amazing how fast this happens. The whole chrysalis develops in about 90 minutes. Yikes, another one has escaped and I find him climbing up my screen.*

*It is clear I need another enclosure so I cut out the bottom out of a plastic pitcher and use the fine screen of an embroidery hoop on the top and bottom so the pillars will have plenty of air and so I can clean out the poop more easily. Good God!*

*Over a thousand people have now seen Sandy's caterpillar cam and someone posts that raising caterpillars makes their work seem easy.*

*No kidding! It would have been different if I had planned to raise them and was prepared. This learn as you go stuff is nuts!*

*Note to self. This is amazing to watch as you do your caterpillar chores. Just remember this labor of love is worth all the effort! Grandkids are gonna love it tomorrow!!*

# CHAPTER 28
# The Race is on!
# Plum Island
*July 29, 2018*

*"The Race is On!"*

July 29 was a perfect summer day. The heat and humidity had finally abated and towering cumulus clouds provided just enough shade to keep the temperatures in the low Eighties.

It was high tide when I met twenty citizen scientists from Essex County Greenbelt, one of the most effective land conservation organizations in the state. It has preserved several thousand acres of land, including some of the marshland leading into Plum Island.

I hadn't taken a close look at the north end of the island for two months and was delighted to see a natural berm had attached to the beach, so the beach had grown thirty feet since the last time we measured it in June.

This was a good sign, but not a great sign. The same thing had happened the summer before. But when the erosion season had commenced in August, long period waves had started to attack the berm and by October it was gone and waves were attacking the base of the dunes themselves. Then, in about eight months the dunes receded over 70 feet back and gone from 30 feet to less than 7 feet tall.

The south end of North Beach looked a little better. A spur of the south jetty that jutted into the Merrimack River was almost entirely covered with sand, and the cove between the spur and the houses on Northern Reservation Terrace had filled in as well. The houses were also protected by dunegrass and the artificial dune that the city, state and residents had built in the late spring.

But the big question was, would the artificial dune provide enough time for the beach to start growing so it could protect the houses naturally, or would the ocean undermine them first? That would depend on what happened on our next stop, the ocean side of the South Jetty.

I was surprised to see that during July's 9-foot high king tides, the combined height of the tide and waves had been sufficient to wash a slurry of sand through the jetty.

It was a reminder that the erosion season would soon be on us. As soon as long period waves from distant hurricanes started reaching these shores the erosion season would begin and only end with the last Northeaster in March.

It would be a long nine months to see if erosion or accretion would win. The race was on.

# CHAPTER 29
# The Dragonfly Mystery
# Plum Island
*July 30, 2018*

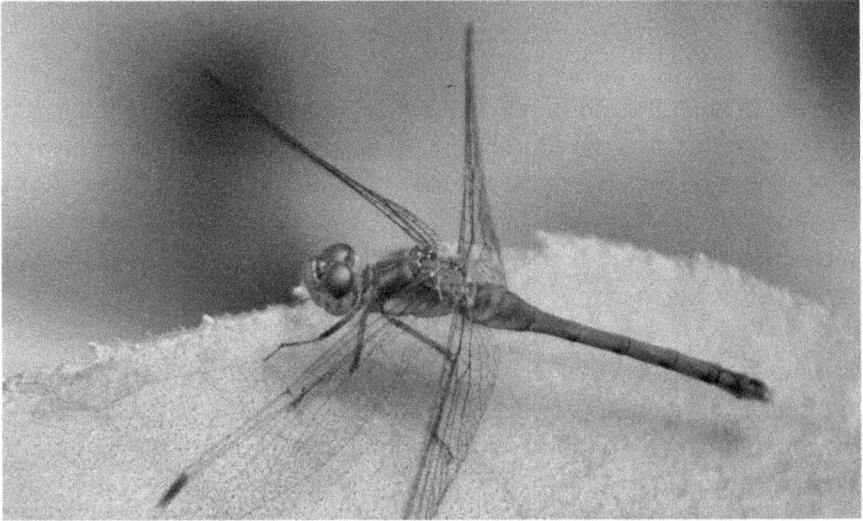

*Yellow-legged meadowhawk Sandy Tilton photo.*

*"For the animal shall not be measured by man. In a world far older and more complete than ours, they move finished and complete. Gifted with the extension of the senses we have lost or never attained, living by voices we shall never hear. They are not brethren, they are not underlings; they are other nations, caught with ourselves in the net of life and time, fellow passengers of the splendid travail of the earth."*
~Henry Beston, The Outermost House

On July 31 I walked out on the first Parker River Wildlife Refuge overlook. A pair of paddle boarders had cavorted with what looked like a Minke whale in front of the overlook the day before.

But what really caught my attention was the nervous rustling of hundreds of clattering dry dragonfly wings. I found myself surrounded with scores of the darting, hovering, shimmering creatures. I could see their bulbous eyes and as they flew by in swarms of glittering light. I felt like I was standing in the middle of a museum diorama depicting, "Life in a Carboniferous swamp, 300 million years ago."

In 2012 a swarm of the same species of dragonflies had cornered a thirty-foot ball of flying mosquitoes between some trees and the side of our house. The dragonflies were hovering around the periphery of the ball keeping the mosquitoes bunched up together. Then, one by one the dragonflies would dart through the ball catching the mosquitoes in their huge basket-like jaws. Then they would bite the mosquitoes in the head to kill them, tear off their wings and use their toothed mouthparts to slash back and forth tearing the hapless mosquitoes into tiny digestible fragments.

I happened to be wearing sunglasses so I could see the polarized light being reflected off the dragonfly's gossamer wings. It is interesting that the dragonflies were doing the same thing. They also had vision that allowed them to see the polarized light shimmering off the wings of the flying mosquitoes. In addition they had compound eyes made up of 28,000 simple eyes called ommatidia that allowed them to detect motion in all directions.

These were wandering glider dragonflies, <u>Pantala flavescens</u> on their late summer migration to the Gulf of Mexico. A few years before, I had witnessed scores of tree-inch long green darner Anax dragonflies doing the same thing on a beach in Marblehead. They had collected on the coast in preparation for flying to their next stop, but a cold front had blown them prematurely out to sea and they were struggling to fly back to the safety of the beach. There they were collecting on the wrackline to feed on what looked like immature sand fleas.

After feeding at this way station these dragonflies will fly to the end of Plum Island where they will wait for propitious winds and fly over Plum Island Sound to Crane's Beach. They will continue this hopscotch pattern until they or their offspring reach the Gulf of Mexico. Possibly they fly as far as South America where the same species is also present. At this point we are not sure of exactly where this American migration begins and ends.

Recently, however, scientists have discovered that this same species of wandering glider dragonfly holds the all-time distance record for insect migration. Dr. Charles Anderson had lived in the Maldive Islands since 1983. But a few years ago he noticed a huge influx of wandering glider dragonflies. This was very odd. He knew that dragonflies need fresh water ponds to raise their families, but as a marine biologist he knew that the Maldive Islands are composed of sand so any rainwater that falls on them is quickly absorbed.

Apparently the dragonflies were migrating to the island from some place else, so he started noting the dates when the dragonflies arrived in the Maldive Islands around October and comparing them to when swarms of the insects were seen in India.

Sure enough the dragonflies were flying down India's coast then waiting for the high altitude winds that follow the monsoons and riding them 3,000 feet in the air to Sri Lanka and the Maldive Islands.

But that was not all. He also found that after leaving the Maldive Islands, swarms of the same dragonflies arrived in East Africa, 8,700 miles away! This makes theirs the longest migration of any insect in the world, almost twice as long as those of monarch butterflies.

Ancestors of these dragonflies probably started making these migrations 350 million years ago when India, Africa, Sri Lanka and the Maldive Islands were all bunched up together. As the continents drifted apart these determined dragonflies just kept expanding their migrations further and further south.

So the main mystery had been solved but the details still have to be filled in. Exciting stuff!

# CHAPTER 30
# Metamorphosis
# Seabrook, NH
*August 8, 2018*

*The butterfly is about to hatch out of its chrysalis. Sandy Tilton photo.*

When we last left Sandy's caterpillars they had just shed their skins and become beautiful green chrysalises. They looked like jade jewelry boxes with a frieze of shiny gold buttons running down their sides.

If you are like me you probably think that caterpillars do something like go into a cocoon-like changing room, change costumes and emerge as fluttering butterflies — a bit like dancers at the Bolshoi Ballet.

But the real story is actually one of the most profound life events on the face of our planet. Inside its chrysalis the first caterpillar had released enzymes that were dissolving its own tissues and leaving behind a soupy mix of amorphous protoplasm. If you had cut into the pupa at this stage all that would have oozed out would have been a dark brown fluid and you, of course, would have killed the future butterfly.

But certain highly organized groups of cells can survive the digestive enzymes. These imaginal discs form when the caterpillar is still developing inside its egg. It grows a disc for each body part it will need as an adult, a disc for the wings, eyes, feet, antennae and all its other future organs.

It is important that the caterpillar has eaten its own skin, and sometimes even the last caterpillar to hatch, so his protoplasm soup will be rich with his brothers' proteins. The imaginal discs will then proceed to use this soup to fuel the rapid cell division required to form the wings, antennae, legs and eyes of an almost entirely new organism. And the discs will have accomplished all this in less than ten days. One study even suggests that a butterfly can remember what it learned as a caterpillar, before it was digested!

Of course this rapid division of cells sounds eerily familiar. It is the same process that happens during cancer. If researchers could figure out how the imaginal discs keep this process under control, they would probably gather up a few nice big fat Nobel Prizes and come close to finding that other elusive prize a definitive cure for cancer.

On August 8 it finally happened. A seam appeared on the chrysalis and the long legs of a male butterfly reached outside the case and held on as the body slid out of the chrysalis. It would have fallen to the floor if the bedraggled butterfly had not been hanging on.

Then the butterfly pulled himself up onto the empty chrysalis and let his wings unfold like a wet accordion. In less than a minute he was fully free and only the skin of the chrysalis remained. It would take a few more hours for the butterfly's wings to dry and for him to start flying around inside Sandy's closed-in porch.

Sandy mused, should she call in sick or request maternity leave? Nope her boss wasn't going to fall for any of that, so she dutifully trudged off to work.

But when she got home she found #1 butterfly stuck in the bottom of a drinking glass so she coaxed it onto a stick and released it in her garden of rudekia and butterfly bushes.

This was the first step in a migration that would take the butterfly down the coast and around the Gulf of Mexico to the conifer forests of Central Mexico. Not bad for a creature that weighs a bit less than a cricket!

But Sandy's saga was far from over. Her field notes pick up the story.

**9 August 2018.**
*Today I almost threw out the baby with the bath water. The butterflies seem to have an internal clock that tells them to hatch out at about 8am. So I filmed #2 emerge but had to cover its enclosure to go to work at 8:30. But when I returned home I found it had flown the coop as well.*

*I had made plans to meet Rochelle Joseph and release the butterfly at Plum Island's Pink House, but this case of the missing Monarch changed everything.*

*So I decided to throw out some of the trash from the day before and lo and behold I found tiny #11 crawling around on the bottom of the trash where he had been happily munching on old milkweed leaves, safe from his voracious brothers. I had almost thrown him out.*

*But #2 was still on the lam. So I decided to just sit down, fix myself a cocktail and see if he would show up. Sure enough he did so I put him out where I had released #1 the day before.*

*He seemed to be waiting for something and sure enough, a minute later #1 came fluttering by and tapped his brother on the head as if to welcome him to the new world.*


Humans like to anthropomorphize about large creatures that we can identify with but do so far less about creatures like a butterflies that just seems to flit about aimlessly like Dory in the movie Finding Nemo. How could such a seemingly haphazard flyer migrate over three thousand miles to Central Mexico?

But we now know that they do, and we even know that several butterflies released from the Monarch Garden in Ipswich were found on the same conifer tree in the Mexican Mountain. So it doesn't seem so far fetched that #1 and #2 really had searched each other out and would feel more comfortable flying beside each other on their migration south.

This led to a dilemma. Would it be better if Sandy stuck to her original plan and release the rest of the butterflies on Plum Island? Or would the butterflies prefer it if they were all released together so they all migrate in tandem to Mexico?

But Sandy had learned that Murphy's Law applies to raising almost any animal. Anything that can go wrong will go wrong and better to just see what nature wants you to do, and then play it by ear.

# CHAPTER 31
# Dead Seals
# Sandy Point
*August 15, 2018*

*Seagulls feasting on PCB laden seal.*

August 15 was another hot, humid day. A miasma of fetid fog hung just offshore and the wrackline was sickly pink as far as the eye could see.

Four days before, torrents of rain had overwhelmed the urban sewage plants in Lowell, Lawrence, Haverhill Manchester and Nashua so the managers had released tens of millions of gallons of raw sewage along with storm water runoff into the Merrimack River.

And now we were seeing the results. In the absence of sunshine the normally red invasive alga that the storm had pushed ashore had taken on this preternaturally pink color that made it look like someone had poured Pepto-Bismol on the beach. As it decomposed, the water it sat in had become black and anaerobic, overlain with filaments of fungus and white Beggiatea bacteria emitting the odor of rotten eggs.

All coastal towns in Massachusetts are required to test their shellfish beds for E-coli after such rain events. But E-coli is just a proxy for all the other fecal germs that can wash into our coastal waters during storms.

So we were walking through a petri dish of potential germs; Streptococcus viridians, Streptococcus pneumonia. Staphylococcus aureus, Campylobacters pylori and innumerable viruses including those that cause avian flu and distemper perhaps from dog feces that were also washed into the river in the storm water runoff, or transported in such fetid air.

These germs can all produce skin rashes, ear infections, dysentery and more serious conditions like pneumonia, hepatitis, encephalitis and meningitis. It is no wonder that ER admissions in Merrimack Valley Hospitals spike after such events.

You would think we could do better than this; thirty-seven years after President Nixon signed the Clean Waters Act. All communities should have been compliant decades ago.

But then the reports of dead and decomposing harbor seals started to pour in. Thirty dead seal pups in Southern Maine, five on Salisbury Beach, four at the mouth of the Merrimack River, eight on Crane's beach, one on Pavilion Beach and two in Gloucester.

The least decomposed bodies seemed to have beached in the north and the most decomposed ones further south, so the locus of the disease must have been in Maine. So I expected to see some seals on Sandy Point. But what I didn't expect to experience first was the stench of rotting flesh. I followed the odor upwind and sure enough there was the seal whose carcass was so decomposed you could hardly make it out in the pile of sickly mush. Even the coyotes who had visited the night before had wisely left it alone.

Of course it is perfectly possible that the algae had just washed ashore naturally and the pollution had not caused the deaths of the seals. But it was certainly suggestive that one of the human borne avian flu type diseases or one of the pet borne diseases like distemper had run rampant through the seal pup population perhaps when they had still been concentrated in their nurseries.

In Maine, several minke whales had died earlier in the year from avian flu and seals had been decimated years before from what turned out to be distemper from dogs.

Whatever the reason, I decided to take a nice, long, hot soapy shower before going to bed.

# CHAPTER 32
## The Silver Lining
*August 17, 2018*

*Nature constructs a perfect seawall out of algae washed up into a berm during a winter storm. Sandy Tilton photo.*

The midsummer storm with its attendant algae bloom and seal die off had one totally unexpected silver lining.

When I posted the photographs of the long pink wrackline of decaying vegetation, one correspondent pointed out that the seaweed grows naturally offshore and that it always washed in after you had a prolonged easterly storm.

He had obviously been fishing here for sometime and observed nature closely. But it still seemed strange I had never seen algae come ashore in such prodigious quantities.

Another correspondent remembered that the Boston Globe had carried an article in 2012, about an invasive seaweed that had arrived from Japan in the ballast tanks of a ship that had emptied its tanks in Rhode Island. Since then the algae had been spreading rapidly north. Most of the time it grows offshore in profusion because of coastal nutrification but we only see it after storms wash it ashore.

During last March's last storm the alga had created a two to three foot high almost impenetrable wall of thickly tangled hairline membranes interspersed with twigs and leaves. Fortunately nobody decided to remove the wall, which would have been almost impossible anyway.

I assumed the wall would gradually break down during the summer. But here it was, still two feet high and almost a mile long as it wrapped around Sandy Point.

But the fascinating thing was that an equally thick wall of sea milkwort was growing on top of the wall and sand had filled in behind it. Nature had made an almost perfect seawall that could absorb the energy of the strongest wave without collapsing.

She had already created a new primary dune protecting the old secondary dune behind. Wind would continue building this primary dune until it formed a formidable bulwark for Sandy Point's future growth. This never would have happened before the invasive species arrived only five years ago.

If humans had built such a seawall it would have cost several million dollars and not worked nearly as well as what Nature had crafted out of an invasive species during a four-day blow in March. Perhaps some of our local environmental engineers should drive down to Sandy Point to pick up some new ideas.

# CHAPTER 33
# Shark Attack!
# Sandy Point
*August 15. 2018*

When I took photos of a decomposed seal on August 15, I assumed it was one of the seals killed by a virus. But after I posted the photos Mike Morris sent a photo of the same seal taken three days before it was so decomposed.

You could see several large shark bite marks on the body and where the shark had crushed the seal's ribs. Then the shark had torn off the seal's head leaving only the lower jaw behind. Mike said the bite marks were similar to ones he had seen from attacks in the area before. It just goes to show you usually see what expect to see, not what is really there!

Several years before, a fisherman was standing in the water watching a seal play off Plum Island's North Point when a shark attacked the seal sending the fisherman clambering up the steep dune in his bulky waders, all to the delight of the other fishermen on the beach, who didn't believe him. They made him the butt of their jokes until several more seals were found with similar bite marks from a Great White Shark.

Mike was something of a shark attack expert himself. Early one morning he was surfing off Plum Island when a Great White Shark had bashed the bottom of his board leaving teeth prints that matched the size of those found on dead seals the following day.

And a few days before I had taken the photo of the dead seal, two paddle boarders had been cavorting with some Humpback whales as they fed on menhaden in front of the houses on Plum Island. Right in the middle of this feeding frenzy was a large triangular dorsal fin. Local experts insisted it was the fin of a basking shark, but that didn't make much sense. Basking sharks feed primarily on plankton. But guess what? Menhaden are one of Great White sharks' favorite food items.

Then, the same day I took the photos, a man was standing in the water 30 yards off Cape Cod's Newcomb's Hollow Beach when a shark tore into his torso. He was rushed to the hospital where he presented in good condition, but was later downgraded to fair condition. That afternoon fishermen reported seeing a Great White Shark in the mouth of the Merrimack River.

All these sharks had probably been born in a Great White shark nursery ground off New York City, which somehow seems fitting. About 20 years ago one of the young female sharks from the nursery swam north and discovered nice fat gray seals rolling around in the shallow waters off Chatham. She started preying on the seals and news of the new food source spread by word of mouth, as it were. The seals were plentiful because the Marine Mammal Act had made seal bounties illegal.

But global warming has heated the ocean temperatures enough so that menhaden now swim regularly north around the biological barrier we call Cape Cod. We had seen the results all summer. The water temperature was about seven degrees higher than usual and Right, Humpback and Minke whales were feeding just off the beach beside striped bass and tuna that were also feeding on the now abundant menhaden. The larger fish had trapped the menhaden against the shore and chased some into fresh water rivers where the menhaden had died from lack of oxygen.

The Great White Sharks are perched at the very apex of this food pyramid. They were feeding on the seals, striped bass and menhaden and were not above taking an exploratory nip out of an occasional human swimmer. This is what happens when you throw nature out of whack. She fights back to reestablish a new equilibrium under the different new conditions.

# CHAPTER 34
# Rip Tide!
# Seabrook Beach
*August 19, 2018*

*Rescuers taking victim off the beach. Salisbury. Sandy Tilton photo.*

A mid-summer storm had raised the seas along Seabrook Beach on August 19. Three-foot high waves kept piling up water along the shore. It had to go somewhere so it set up longshore currents flowing next to the beach. But when those currents encountered a gap in the sandbar that parallels this shore they turned abruptly out to sea, setting up a rip current so strong that it was impossible to swim against. If you get caught in one these currents, the best thing to do is swim parallel to the shore until you get out of the current and can swim back to the beach in calmer waters.

On August 19 Michael Cote and his wife Laura were wading waist deep on Salisbury Beach, but suddenly a rip current swept them hundreds of yards offshore. Matt Tomaskewski saw it happen, grabbed a paddleboard and swam out to help.

First he encountered three swimmers clinging to a surfboard. Michael was already unconscious so Matt did his best to keep Michael's head out of water and to push his torso onto the board, while the other swimmers hung on as best they could.

But then a wave washed Michael's inert body off the surfboard. They tried to paddle out to reach him but the rip current was too strong so Matt told the two other swimmers to stay with the board and use it to catch a wave back to shore.

That left Matt out in the ocean without a paddleboard and he kept losing sight of Michael, who was drifting rapidly out to sea. Matt realized he was too tired to continue further and started swimming back to shore when he met John Giarrusso, a Seabrook police officer who had paddling out on the same board Matt had used before.

John, aided by lifeguards who had shot down on jet skis from Hampton Beach, were able to pull all seven swimmers out of the water. But Michael Cote was pronounced dead on arrival at the Anna Jacques Hospital. The next day Laura Cote was pronounced dead at the Portsmouth Hospital, making their two young daughters the most recent victims of rip tides that are preventable and kill far more swimmers than sharks.

# CHAPTER 35
# Environmental Disaster Strikes
# The Northwest Atlantic Ocean
## *August 22, 2018*

*A seagull feasts on a PCB laden dead seal.*

On August 22 the National Oceanographic and Atmospheric Administration released its preliminary report on what it was now calling a seal die-off.

The report stated that over 400 seals had died, and that the stranding organizations were so overwhelmed they had stopped taking in dead seals so as not to spread any further infection. And that contract scientists were testing the seals' tissues for the most likely suspects, avian flu and phocine distemper. The number of dead seals has since been changed to over a thousand.

Both diseases could account for the sneezing, coughing and severe seizures exhibited by the stranded seals. Although the government scientists were being cautious it was clear that this was arguably the largest environmental disaster to ever hit the Northwest Atlantic Ocean. 20,000 seals had died in the Northeast Atlantic, decades before.

But marine biologist Susan Shaw thought there was a lot more to the story than what NOAA was letting on. In 2011 she had discovered extremely high levels of PCB's in gray and harbor seals, even though the immune suppressing chemicals used in electronics had been banned in 1979.

Because chemicals had been banned, research on them had been largely abandoned as well. But that didn't mean the chemicals had disappeared. They had continued to bio-accumulate as they worked their way up through the food chain from plankton, to fish to higher predators like seals and sharks.

So now, after decades of such dosing, seals were being born with compromised immune systems and the condition only became worse as the young pups suckled their mothers' milk and started eating fish. This made them susceptible to any passing virus or bacteria they would normally be able to ward off.

Although research on PCB's had largely stopped, a handful of scientists like Dr. Shaw had continued to research the orphaned area of study in her own private research facility, Maine's Shaw Institute.

But now the chickens had come home to roost and this was Dr. Shaw's best chance to make the point that the underlying reason for the die-offs of seals was that humans had introduced PCB's into the environment for decades and that the chemicals had continued to accumulate in animals because they were so difficult to metabolize.

She explained that virtually the entire population of gray and harbor seals in the Northwest Atlantic were now susceptible to airborne infectious diseases like avian flu and phocine distemper. But other air breathing marine mammals like finback and minke whales had succumbed as well.

What was potentially even more alarming was that a great white shark had also washed up dead on the beach in Truro. Had it picked up a virus from feeding on infected seals?

This would mean that this environmental tragedy could continue to cascade through the food chain and become the new normal in future years. Only a thorough investigation of the underlying causes of this massive die-off would tell, and it was unclear whether NOAA was willing to do such a study.

# CHAPTER 36
## Full Moon Over Crane's Beach
### *August 26, 2018*

*Full Moon Over Crane's Beach. Sandy Tilton photo.*

The moon had been my constant companion throughout this past year of discovery. I had watched it create extreme low tides and reach down to paint fanciful murals with a palette of black, white and purple garnet sand. So it only seemed fitting to trek out to Crane's Beach to see the last full moon of this extraordinary summer.

I watched transfixed as it rose majestically out of the thin haze over the Atlantic Ocean and saw the planets emerge — first Venus, then Mars, then the stars of the big dipper. Slaves called this same celestial assortment of stars the drinking gourd and used it to guide them north toward freedom.

It was a bit of a shock when I realized that exactly fifty years ago I had been studying monkeys on an island off Puerto Rico and had trekked into the jungly interior to find the monkeys all lined up on a ridge. It was not too far fetched to think that they were waiting for the moon to rise and knew exactly when it would.

Two months before we had watched the moon as Neil Armstrong strode across its surface, then turned his camera back on the earth and we saw it hanging in space; fragile, blue and incredibly beautiful. We knew that the onionskin layer of blue and green contained the continents, the oceans and all the microbes, dinosaurs, plants, hominids and our 5,000 years of civilization.

The nature writer Diane Ackermann reminds us that it was also on such a night that St. Francis was out taking an evening stroll when the moon rose out of the east and lay down a great swath of golden light on the streets of Assisi. Beholding this wonder all alone, he raced into the duomo and started wildly ringing its bells. This usually signaled some kind of disaster, so Assisi's citizens ran into the streets and looked up to find St Francis extolling them, "Lift up your eyes my friends and look at the moon!"

But we were watching the moon rising perceptibly against the black velvet of the sky and noticed something was terribly wrong. The full moon was blood red like those painted by Turner when Iceland's Mount Hekla volcano was spreading ash across the face of Europe.

But our moon was red because of smoke from forest fires in California. It was a reminder that we were witnessing the deterioration of that thin skin of the earth that has made it habitable for over three billion years and which we have managed to decimate since the Industrial Revolution. Is that the reason we have not been able to find other forms of intelligent life in the universe? Is there something in industrial societies that drives them toward destroying the very planets that brought them so far?

# CHAPTER 37
# Humpbacks and Menhaden
# Salisbury Beach
*September 7, 2018*

*Humpback whale feeding on menhaden. Diane Seavey photo.*

Diane Seavey was relieved the temperatures had dropped from the high Nineties to the comfortable Seventies and didn't mind the overcast skies. She had already spent the last four or five days trying to get a decent shot of whales feeding off Salisbury Beach and she didn't have much time. Hurricane Florence was bearing down on the Southeast coast and its waves would cool the surface waters, sending the schools of menhaden or "pogies" the whales were feeding on back south.

Diane had torn her medial collateral cartilage ten days before, so she was wearing a heavy knee brace. She also had a doctor's appointment that was about two hours away and she knew she wouldn't be able to get back to the beach for several days because she had to return to work at the Concord Hospital. She was a food ambassador who helped fifty patients order their meals. Then she had to push the sixty-pound food cart up and down the halls covering almost three miles a day.

Hampered by her brace and encumbered with a heavy tripod and long lens, she hobbled down to the beach and set up a small folding chair near the Seaglass Restaurant.

The wind made it challenging to see where the whales were in the waves. They just kept swimming back and forth only blowing or showing an occasional fin.

"I decided to move down the beach where Sandy Tilton had seen them before. But the whales still just breached on either side and never in front of me."

"Time was running out and I had to make that doctors' appointment but as I was leaving the island I decided to make one more try at access lot #6 where I had had OK luck the day before."

"I attached my camera to the tripod, set up my chair and just sat and watched as the whales breached to the left and the right. I had less than an hour left and I was like 'please, please I just want one good shot.'"

"The next thing I knew a whale was right in front of me and I'm in my view finder watching the pogies bubble up in front of him. I was focusing on how many pogies there were, not realizing that just outside my range of vision the whales were lunging up after the pogies. "

"I probably missed eight or nine shots. I was really upset, so I decided to keep my left eye open while continuing to look through the view finder with my right eye. "

"As soon as I saw the pogies boil up to the surface I zoomed back and suddenly there was a whale swimming and lunge fishing directly at me from only 30 feet away. I could see his pink tongue and baleen plates and hundreds of pogies cascading out of his huge mouth. It was pretty exciting and I was just hoping the shots would come out and be in focus and you have the results!"

# CHAPTER 38
## Shark Attack
## Newcomb's Hollow, Wellfleet
### *September 15, 2018*

*Great White Shark. Hans Morris.*

On September 15 a Great White Shark killed a young man boogie boarding near the old life saving station on Wellfleet's Newcomb's Hollow Beach. It was the first fatal shark attack in Massachusetts in 83 years.

But it was not really a surprise. The population of seals had been steadily increasing since the enactment of the Marine Mammal Protection Act in 1972 and the population of Great White sharks had followed suit. The ecosystem was now clearly out of balance.

The sharks had started to swim in close to the beach to attack seals and even to eye children running on the dry sand. The older sharks seemed to have pushed the younger sharks from the center of their feeding territory centered on Cape Cod to the North Shore on the periphery of their feeding territory.

It was also possible that the rapid loss of thousands of seals due to porcine distemper had made the sharks more aggressive and hungrier.

The attacks had become more frequent in recent years. In 2014 a shark bit a swimmer on Cape Cod and in August a shark had almost killed a swimmer in Truro. It had been merely a matter of time before a shark actually killed someone. Since most of the Cape Cod's Great White sharks are tagged it is possible that scientists know if one rogue shark or several were to blame for the attacks.

Less expected was the discovery of the body of a two-year-old humpback whale floating dead in the water off Gloucester. Unfortunately it had initially appeared to have the same markings as the two-year-old whale that so many people had photographed feeding off Salisbury Beach. Then another minke whale washed up dead on the beach in nearby Rye, New Hampshire

If the whales died from phocine distemper like all the seals and four other minke whales, plus a finback and another Humpback whale, it would show that those infections had spread to other species.

But Hurricane Florence was on the way and it was uncertain whether researchers could retrieve the body and if they did it would take several months to get the results of any autopsy. It was just the coda of another long strange summer of climate change.

The menhaden fishery also returned because of good regulations. It is the largest fishery in the world and traditionally produces poultry food, which was why your Purdue chicken used to taste so fishy.

Now most of the menhaden catch goes into producing Omega -3 fish oil pills, and farmers have switched to feeding their chicken soybeans because of American tariffs.

So who says President Trump hasn't done anything for the country? Chicken now tastes fatty, just how he likes 'em.

Several years ago the Atlantic States Fisheries Commission established quotas for how many menhaden could be caught by each state and for the past three years there have been so many menhaden that whales have started swimming inshore to feast on them.

Whales and seals were protected by the Marine Mammal and the Endangered Species acts. And of course Great White sharks have returned because of the abundance of seals.

So now people don't have to spend thousands of dollars travelling to Africa to see an apex predator kill prey. They can watch from the safety of their own beach.

In an era when scientists are warning that over a million species could go extinct in the next few decades it is reassuring that we have been able to return the Atlantic coast to a semblance of what it was like in Pre-colonial times when whales were common along these shores.

But I suppose we will soon be trying to decide what to do about problem ospreys that nest on baseball field lighting fixtures and Great White sharks that take curious nips out of occasional swimmers that venture too far into the sharks' natural feeding territories.

All these successes are the fruition of environmental acts passed in the Seventies by that great softhearted hippy environmentalist, Richard M. Nixon. We should thank him for his foresight... I think.

# CHAPTER 39
# The Whale; Seabrook Beach
## *August 13, 2019*

*Humpback whale feeding on menhaden. Sandy Tilton.*

August 13 broke warm and sultry. The rising sun was hidden behind thick offshore fogbanks. All that could be seen was a vast expanse of light gray sky above equally gray waters.

Two screaming osprey soared overhead until one them folded her wings and plunged into the water to surface with a wriggling fat menhaden firmly grasped in her talons.

Hopefully she would not be mugged by a wayward bald eagle that Benjamin Franklin famously declared were birds of low morale values compared to turkeys that had the sagacity to outrun predators and should thus be our national symbol.

But osprey have their own sagacity. Soon the two osprey will fly south to overwinter, one in Florida the other two states away. In the spring they will return to nest in Seabrook again because they mate for life. They have learned that the way to maintain a good marriage is to take separate winter vacations, I suppose.

Suddenly the surface waters start to dimple from the fins of menhaden and the huge black head of a Humpback whale surfaces in front of the grayness and rises majestically higher as hundreds of foot-long menhaden jump clear of his gaping maw.

Human fishermen are casting for striped bass lurking below the thick schools of menhaden that darkened the water with their abundance. The head of a large Gray seal looks curiously from close to shore where it feels safer from the predations of a Great White Shark that has been patrolling the waters from Cape Ann to New Hampshire all summer long.

In Annisquam researchers from the National Marine Fisheries Service had been leaning over the edge of an inflatable Zodiak trying to free a Minke whale when the harbormaster in a nearby boat frantically radioed:

"Let go of the line and back away as quickly as possible."

Two seconds later a Great White Shark slammed into the flank of the whale, which broke it free of the entangling lobster gear. But it swam away streaming a trail of blood gushing from a two-foot wide bite mark in its once sleek torso.

Now, a menhaden boat sets a huge seine around a school of menhaden only yards from the whale and a tiny lone kayaker holding two triangular sails aloft to keep up with the whale looks on with curiosity and what seems to be, dare I say it, affection.

This feeding frenzy is a vivid example of an accelerated flow of nutrients up through a food chain.

Two nights ago, part of the menhaden had been a ton of inorganic matter lying on the ocean floor. Yesterday morning they had been converted to thousands of pounds of phytoplankton. By afternoon they had been consumed and transformed into thousands of pounds of menhaden muscle. This morning they were being metabolically converted into hundreds of pounds of whale blubber.

Certainly this is a food chain rapid and simple enough to grasp; inorganic matter to primary producer to consumer to predator in four easy steps.

But the frenzy is also the result of five major conservation successes. In the Seventies there had only been 10 pairs of nesting osprey from Canada to New York. Now there are close to a thousand pairs in Massachusetts alone.

# CHAPTER 40
# Eastern Equine Encephalitis
# Ipswich, Massachusetts
### September 16, 2019

Throughout the summer of 2019 I noticed flocks of egrets flying over my house at dusk. I mentioned this to a neighbor who told me they were on their way to a hidden rookery. But you could just see it from the top of a neighboring hill.

I drove to the hill and looked down into a heavily wooded valley. But one copse looked like all its trees were covered with white sheets. I figured if I drove down the hill I should be able to get close enough to take a few photographs.

Sure enough I found a cul de sac and a path that lead to a swampy pond. I peered through a screen of vegetation and saw that the trees around the pond were covered with hundreds of Snowy Egrets, Great Egrets and Great Blue Herons.

Guano from the birds had killed most of the trees and the pond was covered with a fetid scum of blue green algae. All that I could hear were prehistoric kronks and grunts that made me think a Velociraptor was peering at me from the other side of the vegetation.

Toward the end of the summer the resident birds were joined by more egrets from Maine and Canada. They spent the day gorging themselves on minnows and frogs from the surrounding marshes and then would gather at the rookery for the night. By the end of the summer close to 400 birds flew into the rookery every evening.

I started going to the spot at dusk to take photos of the birds against the late summer sunsets. It was difficult for the large birds to avoid the trees that surrounded the pond so they would sideslip and stall as they made their descents down through the vegetation to finally settle on a few tall gangly sumac trees.

I made a point of wearing long clothes and drenching myself with DEET but every night I was bitten by a few mosquitoes. I realized I was doing everything wrong.

I was going out at dusk when the mosquitoes were most active. I was standing beside the fetid pond where they laid their eggs and I was around hundreds of birds that the mosquitoes were infecting with Eastern Equine Encephalitis. The media was starting to carry stories about Triple E but I knew that it was rare and most of the cases were in other parts of the state.

I figured our mosquitoes probably weren't infected and getting a photo of a flock of egrets flying against a Wagnerian sunset was surely worth a few mosquito bites. I thought I was playing the odds. I was actually playing a game of Russian roulette.

On September 16th I started feeling lousy.
I hadn't slept very well the night before and I woke up with a headache, fever and chills. I had just finished a long bout of difficult writing and felt that I just needed some sleep but the next morning I read that Essex County had just gone on high alert because a man in neighboring Manchester had contracted EEE and would be dead within the week.

OK this was serious. I berated myself for being so foolhardy and checked into a clinic hoping they would ell me I was just being paranoid. Instead they drew blood and set up tests for EEC, Ehrlichiosis, Lyme disease and Babesia. The results would come back within a week.

Our local clinic doesn't fool around with these arboviruses. Two thirds of the people who live on some of our town's streets have tick borne diseases and Massachusetts consistently has more cases of EEC than any other state in the nation. We already had 10 cases this year; almost a third of them would prove to be fatal.

I did some research and discovered that like tick borne diseases, EEE is on the rise. Normally there are only an average of 7 cases of EEC a year nationwide. This year there had already been 28 cases of EEE and Massachusetts led the way with 10 cases. The disease would prove to be fatal a third of the time in humans and 90% of the time in horses.

In fact this was the worst year for EEE since the CDC first started reporting on the disease in the early Sixties. It also turns out that from the beginning most of the work on EEE has been done by the U.S. army.

The disease was only discovered sixty years ago and during the Sixties the army had a cocktail of three similar agents sitting in an Olympic sized swimming pool in the Pine Bluff Arsenal in Arkansas. There, to be sprayed over Cuba in the event the United States decided to invade Cuba to rid the island of Soviet missiles.

The idea was that Cuban soldiers would spike a 105 degree fever; come down with searing headache and light sensitivity. The last thing they would want to do is pick up a gun to protect their motherland.

Like the Plum Island Animal Disease Research Laboratory, the Pine Bluff Arsenal also had an insectary. It is known researchers infected fleas with biological agents at the site. Had they also infected mosquitoes with EEE and had the mosquitoes escaped to infect migrating birds like heron and egrets?

The Department of Defense is still studying EEE because of its potential as a biological weapon and its researchers are being vaccinated with a vaccine developed in one of the Department's military labs. I guess nothing could go wrong with the vaccine against EEE either.

A week later I received my results. I didn't have EEE. Apparently there was a 48-hour bug going around that mimicked EEE's symptoms or that some lucky people only get the minor symptoms. Not much is really known about the disease because it had formerly been so rare.

But I decided I had more than enough photographs of herons and egrets. My friends said that it was ridiculous that our town had sprayed to get rid of the mosquitoes. It made the whole town smell like a pig farm and the mosquitoes would die off as soon as we had two days of killing frosts anyway. They were probably right, but having had a close call, I appreciated our town's proactive stance.

# CHAPTER 41
# Bombogenesis and the Norwegian Dawn
*October 17, 2019*

If subtropical storm Melissa had been like a professionally refereed prizefight between two evenly matched boxers. If she had taken her time slowly wearing down her opponent to win by a judge's decision. Then the bombogenesis storm that followed was like being sucker punched in a dark alley.

Even though the bomb cyclone storm was not given an official name it's ninety per hour winds and extreme low-pressure core set the Massachusetts record for October.

It arrived almost unannounced while New England was still reeling from Melissa. At first it looked like it would pass through so quickly it would cause little damage but as meteorologists rechecked their instruments it became clear that it's short-lived power alone would raise havoc and it did.

Soon higher than forecast winds were toppling trees that still wore their full sets of leaves. They fell through houses and took down power lines leaving close to 500,000 New Englanders in the dark on a Thursday morning. Schools were closed and hundreds of boats were torn from their moorings and strewn willy-nilly over beaches and marshes by waves that had also be underestimated.

In the morning I scoured through several Facebook pages but people were still responding to yesterday's news. Scores of people had posted shots of elegant praying mantises and respondents were curious about why there were so many.

Was it another manifestation of global warming? I finally looked it up and the answer was simple. It was autumn and that's when male mantises actively seek out females. But they have to be careful while they are busily mating on top of the female, the female would reach back, decapitate her oblivious suitor and happily munch his head while his lower extremities continued to procreate.

But one particular sunrise post caught my attention. It showed the vague outlines of a large ship sitting just off Pavilion Beach in Ipswich. Several people questioned the post's veracity because the ship was so conveniently obscured by waves and moisture.

But I remembered seeing a similar thing in Woods Hole. Early one morning I was walking along Nobska Beach and looked up to see the large bulk and elegant lines of the QE2 slipping just offshore. She was on her way to running aground on the Pigs and Sows ledge off the Elizabeth Islands. The passengers had to be off loaded at sea and transported rather unhappily by bus to New York as I remember.

So I jumped into my car and drove down to Pavilion Beach and sure enough there were the two large cruise ships not far offshore. I took some pictures but they weren't very good. The ships were at eye level and the waves were too high and there was too much moisture in the air to see anything clearly.

Later I had to run some early morning errands and realized I was part way to Crane's Beach. Perhaps I could see the ships from a different angle. But neither the guard at the castle nor the parking lot attendant knew about any ships. But I decided to take a look myself and as soon as I topped the boardwalk there they were. They loomed just above where dogs were frolicking on the sand.

The elevation of the boardwalk allowed me to see above the waves and mist so I could even see the ships' names. One was the Norwegian Dawn headed for New York with over two thousand passengers, the other was The Seven Seas Navigator with four hundred passengers bound for Boston. They had both been on their fall foliage cruises and had to dart into Ipswich Bay to wait out the storm before they could get around Cape Ann to transit the Cape Cod Canal.

If we had still been in the age of sail we would have had two shipwrecks and several thousand drowned passengers on our hands. Fortunately the Norwegian vessels had diesel engines and positioning systems so they could jog out the storm in safety.

The last time I had seen something like this was when the El Dia ran aground on Cape Cod's Nauset Beach and was stranded for several weeks creating a welcome mini tourist boom in late March.

When I drove home I realized how fortunate I had been. A cop car blocked my way. If I had not had errands to run I would have taken my regular route and been turned away from venturing further. Mother Nature had shown me the way, once again!

# EPILOGUE
## The Case for Optimism
### *November 14, 2019*

*Menhaden being chased to the surface by a humpback whale. Diane Seavey photo.*

Scenes similar to what Diane Seavey's saw on Salisbury Beach had been occurring up and down New England's shores. Whales were seen feeding on menhaden they had cornered in the mouth of the Merrimack River and in Boston and Beverly Harbors.

In Provincetown, thousands of menhaden died after beaching themselves to escape the jaws of marauding schools of bass, bluefish and humpback whales. Some of the menhaden were able to flip themselves back into the ocean, others to survive in tidepools, but most used up all the available oxygen in the shallow waters and died on what was called Herring Cove Beach which made you think incidents like this had happened there before.

It was easy to see how colonialists and Native Americans before them had been able to hunt whales so close to shore from sturdy dugout canoes. But the menhaden's abundance was also testament to humankind's ability to return an ecosystem to its former abundance.

Menhaden have been called the world's most important fish and they make up the world's largest fisheries. In colonial times their offshore migrations were as large and impressive as those of Buffalo and Passenger Pigeons on land. Their schools were a hundred feet deep and stretched for miles. John Smith wrote that menhaden were so thick he was able to scoop them directly into his frying pan.

Menhaden are the keystone species of the East Coast. They convert trillions of pounds of plankton into millions of pounds of rank oily fish that provides food for hundreds of thousands of pounds of striped bass, bluefish, sharks whales and tuna. They also consume untold quantities of nitrogen and phosphorous rich phytoplankton keeping the oceans free of algal blooms and zones of dead anaerobic mud.

All of this changed after world war two when menhaden seiners started using spotter planes to lead them to the prominent schools and the menhaden fishery became the largest fishery in the world. The main company in the business was Zapata Oil owned by President George Bush Senior. The oily fish were ground up and used to feed chicken, turkeys and hogs.

I like to ask beach goers if they have ever eaten menhaden.

"Why certainly not!"

"Well have you ever eaten a Perdue chicken?"

"Of course!'

"Then I guarantee you have eaten menhaden."

I go on to explain that menhaden are also the reason their chicken is so oily and often smells like fish. By this time I am usually alone on the beach.

Populations of menhaden have recently plummeted because of they are used to make Omega-3 fish oil pills. Their concomitant decline forced the Atlantic States Marine Fisheries Commission to enact quotas for each state on the Atlantic and Gulf coasts.

Massachusetts's seiners are now allowed up to 125,000 pounds of menhaden a trip to fulfill the state's six million pound quota. The fecund little menhaden have done the rest. The regulations show that unlike Buffalo or Passenger pigeons, marine species are so prolific they can recover if given half a chance.

The comeback of menhaden was the capstone of a long strange summer that had seen soaring water temperatures, severe rain events, sewage overflows, human health problems and seals dying from phocine distemper and being exposed from birth to a toxic brew of immune suppressing levels of PCB's.

All these problems are being caused by growing human populations, rampant industrialization and over development of our coasts. But the return of whales and menhaden show that nature is a self-healing system and if humans manage to control our wanton ways our planet can return to the lush abundance of its former days.

www.ingramcontent.com/pod-product-compliance
Lightning Source LLC
Chambersburg PA
CBHW032145020426
42334CB00016B/1227